MW00929756

THE
Last Trolley Stop

Memories of Poverty, Bigotry, and Religiosity in Washington, D.C. and Rural Kentucky during the Great Depression

HEBER BOULAND

Copyright © 2014 by Heber Bouland
All rights reserved.

ISBN: 1500155055
ISBN 13: 9781500155056
Library of Congress Control Number: 2014910791
CreateSpace Independent Publishing Platform
North Charleston, South Carolina

In memory of my parents

Thomas and Epsie Bouland

and

The children of the shanty ghetto

TABLE OF CONTENTS

INTRODUCTION

The crude sign read "No Jews or Italians Allowed." It was nailed to a telephone pole at a popular Chesapeake Bay beach where my family and other Washingtonians played in the 1930s. Blacks in the Washington, D.C. area suffered much greater bigotry than Jews, Italians, or any other ethnic group. My story about poverty, bigotry, religiosity, and other faces of the Great Depression begins in 1933 at the peak of the depression and the year FDR began his presidency. I was five years old, just beginning to have some vague awareness of what was going on outside a childish self-centered life. Our family lived in an unusual middle class neighborhood in NW Washington, D.C. Four doors from us, a U.S. Senator from North Dakota lived in a large, fine house. Two blocks in the opposite direction, five or six black families endured life in one-room shanties without running water or electricity. Most D.C. residents were white Protestants, and most did not suffer during the Great Depression because the New Deal created new government jobs. Hobos rode to town on freight trains looking for handouts and families from Pennsylvania, West Virginia, and rural Maryland moved to D.C. seeking work.

I saw rural poverty on summer visits to my uncle's tobacco farm in western Kentucky where he lived with his elderly mother and three unwed sisters. They lived without indoor plumbing, central heating, phone service, or adequate lighting. Ninety percent of American farms had no electricity and farm prices had fallen by fifty percent since the 1929 stock market crash. I saw white sharecroppers living in one-room shacks much like the black shanties back home.

Over the next decade or so, I witnessed severe poverty and bigotry up close, but experienced little myself, although sometimes I had to put cardboard in my shoes to cover holes in the soles and did experience minor religious bigotry. My mother, who converted from Methodism to become a Seventh-day Adventist (SDA) shortly before I was born, sent or took me to the Adventist church. Members observed the seventh-day Sabbath and many were vegetarians. Neighborhood kids occasionally called us names like, "Seven days grass eaters." In other respects, I had a privileged childhood because periodically we hired domestics to clean our home and a few times I even rode around D.C. in a chauffeur-driven limousine.

When I told one of my grown sons I was writing my childhood memoirs, he pretended to be reading a boring book very slowly. He mocked, "Got…. up….. in…. the…. morning, ate breakfast, went to school." I said, "What if I told about your great uncle having sex with the neighbor's new sixteen year old bride?" He replied, "Oh, sounds like you have a story there." Some material is about humdrum everyday life, but I've tried to capture the heart wrenching pain of the poverty and bigotry of the times— how the shanty children got up in the morning after sleeping on a thin mat on a cold floor, maybe ate a breakfast of dried toast, and walked miles to a small segregated school on legs twisted with rickets from lack of milk. I intermingled the pain with some humorous and naughty stories, as well as anecdotes about the culture of the times, and even the tragic murder of my cousin. People were much more religious back in those days, and I have included some stories about religion, but I like the word religiosity which has the implication of affected piety. While my story focuses on the depression years, I carry some aspects through to today, to show how things played out and the contrast between now and then.

Although I checked some facts and figures on the internet, my story is based primarily on my memories augmented by those of relatives and friends. However, memories of those who lived back then have steadily been lost, as these folks die or their minds malfunction. I regret not starting sooner.

NATION'S CAPITAL FACES POVERTY, BIGOTRY, AND RELIGIOSITY

THE LAST TROLLEY STOP

A bout twenty small World War I open-cockpit biplanes flying in tight formation swept out of the bright southern sky and roared low over our house, their wheels seemed to just miss the tree tops. I was in our backyard playing, while my father raked leaves that had fallen over the winter. It was March 4, 1933, a clear and sunny day, sometime past noon. Next month I would turn five years old.

"What's that?" I asked, startled, excited, and a little afraid. "They're celebrating the inauguration of Mr. Franklin Roosevelt, our new president," my father replied. FDR had won the election four months earlier on a campaign of bold, experimental, and controversial programs to cope with the Great Depression. We lived six miles almost directly north of the capitol building where the president had just been sworn in

When President Roosevelt took the oath of office and gave his famous, "fear itself" speech on the Capitol's East Portico, he faced a large audience, but beyond was the outline of a large slum extending eastward where blacks lived in squalor. Another large ghetto spread northward from the Capitol, (See Figure 1, the map of D.C. during the 1930s). After the inauguration, dignitaries had a luncheon at the Capitol, and this was followed by a big parade with marching bands, floats, and all the works moving along Pennsylvania Avenue toward the White House. On the left side of the avenue were government offices and on the right side or north were commercial offices, hotels, and stores. About halfway along the route between the Capitol and the White House was the commercial city center, downtown Washington, with nearby eight to ten story department stores e.g., Woodies, Hecht's, Kann's, and Palace Royal. There are no skyscrapers here because congress wanted the Capitol to be the most prominent building in the city. Blacks weren't allowed to shop at the department stores and some Christians avoided shopping at Jewish stores. One neighbor advised, "Only shop at Woodies (Woodard & Lothrop) because it's the only department store owned by gentiles, plus they don't hire Jews." My mother ignored the admonition. Several years later Kann's department store was the first one in the city to use black mannequins.

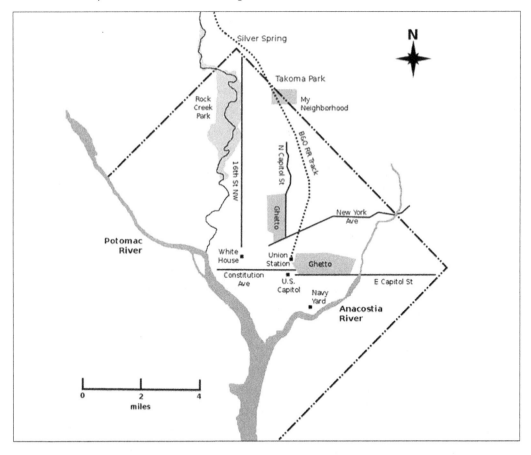

Figure 1. Location of two major downtown black ghettos and my neighborhood in Washington D.C. in the 1930s

When I was four, Mother started taking me shopping with her at these department stores. She often left me in the toy department while she tried on dresses but she didn't buy me any toys. After shopping, we boarded a trolley and headed for home. The trolley we took, originated at the Navy Yard on the Anacostia River where a civilian contractor went on a shooting rampage in 2013 killing twelve people. In the 1930s it was a benign place and the Navy often held open house for the public. I went there once as a youngster and toured a small war vessel, probably a destroyer. After leaving the Navy Yard the trolley went north and near the capitol building turned left or west on Pennsylvania Avenue where my mother and I boarded it in the commercial city center.

Readers, let's go back to the early 1930s and take this trolley ride. The trolley we take is a small electric streetcar with hard cane seats, operated by a motorman, and has a conductor who collects the ten cent fares and pulls a cord which rings a signal bell when passengers are safely on board. As the trolley rolls along the tracks, the motorman clangs a gong to warn

Figure 2. The black ghetto east of the U. S. Capitol (Courtesy D.C. Public Library, Washingtoniana Division)

pedestrians and cars. Our trolley stops every few blocks to discharge or load passengers such as shoppers, domestics, and high level government bureaucrats. The passengers are a mix of rich and poor, black and white, and young and old. While blacks aren't required to sit at the back of the

trolley, most practice voluntary segregation. There are students, even grade school students, riding the trolley. They can ride public transportation to school at a deep discount. While I never rode the trolley to school, when I was ten or eleven I could ride it alone or with my friends to visit downtown museums. Most of the passengers are well dressed; there are no casual clothes in the 1930s. All adults are wearing hats and male office workers wearing three piece suits which are frumpy wool in the winter and crinkly seersucker in the summer. Many of them are carrying a large bulky brown leather brief case with wide straps and buckles. It's probably a government issue. Women are wearing long drab gray, black, or blue

Figure 3. Washington, D.C. slums in 1935 (Source Library of Congress)

dresses, never slacks and seldom skirts and blouses. For male students under twelve the uniform is corduroy knickers and a simple shirt. Girls wear dresses with a simple pattern and which come well below the knees. The conductors and motormen wear black uniforms with brass buttons, a white shirt, and a distinguished black cap. But they usually don't look dignified because the uniforms are a little dirty and wrinkled and the coat unbuttoned. Frequently the trolley is so crowded passengers must stand in the aisles holding onto leather straps.

A few blocks before Pennsylvania Avenue reaches the White House, we turn north on Fourteenth Street, and after traveling through a commercial area, we soon reach residential neighborhoods, where we first see three-story narrow row houses, then wider two-story row houses or duplexes, and finally single family homes. In the individual neighborhoods there are blocks and blocks of houses that look exactly alike. At one point we reach a large trolley barn where trolleys are garaged and serviced. Downtown the trolley power lines are underground, but here they are overhead and our trolley stops over a pit where a pitman disengages the trolley from the underground line and the motorman or conductor gets out and raises a long trolley pole connecting it to the overhead line. Our trolley continues north making a couple of jogs to the east. While the streets are tree lined, most yards are too small to accommodate large trees. We soon reach the last trolley stop—the end of the line for trolleys from downtown D.C. My mother and I step off and walk the few blocks to our house. Sometimes I feel a little squeamish after taking a long stop and go, lurching trolley ride. Our home is on First Street near the northern apex of the city and the Maryland /D.C. line in a community called Takoma Park. Here the scenery is more open and freer. The warm textured wooden homes are distinct, not a duplication of a neighbor's home, and on large lots with tall oak trees and lots of shrubbery giving the community a natural, comfortable, welcome feeling.

Besides having large yards and big oak trees, the life style also distinguished Takoma Park from the city. The last trolley stop community had a large population of Seventh-day Adventists (SDA), a minority religion nationwide. Most didn't smoke, drink, dance, play cards, or go to the movies, and they worshiped on Saturday. But then most of the other residents here were white Anglo Saxon Protestants (WASP's) with names like Peterson,

Rice, Wellman, Shepard, White, and Smith and religions such as Baptist, Methodist, Lutheran, and Presbyterian. Takoma Park was maybe a little puritanical and how did H.L.Mencken define Puritanism? "The haunting fear that someone, somewhere was happy." In any event most Protestants, except for maybe Episcopalians, especially in the 1930s, weren't noted for engaging in fun loving and fast living activities like the southern and eastern Europeans and Irish that lived in the city and who some sterotyped as whiskey drinking gamblers. Maybe I'm exaggerating but for Takoma Park citizens in the 1930s, trimming one's rose bushes, sipping lemonade, and going to the Fourth of July parade or a church social were the big excitements.

Other things made Takoma Park unique and gave it contradictions. The community was located partly in D.C. and partly in two Maryland counties.

Figure 4. The last trolley stop ending at downtown Takoma Park in the 1930s. The church on left played a big part in my early life. (Source, C.W. Witbeck Photo courtesy of National Trolley Museum)

The Maryland side was an incorporated town complete with a mayor and city council while the D.C. section, which was not a formal political unit and the boundary lines were even ambiguous, was governed by the Washington, D.C. commissioners. By the mid-thirties, the community was a middle class or upper middle class area with an unusual mix of large old Victorian homes, many of which had seen better days, and small bungalows. Another Takoma Park irony was that the B&O Railroad line, with several light industrial businesses nearby, ran through the upscale residential neighborhoods. When families bought homes they often signed covenants that they would not resell to "Colored" or "Negros." I've read about covenants that restricted home sales to "White Protestants" or that prohibited home sales to "Members of the Hebrew Race." Yet there were two small black shanty ghettos in the midst of the all-white neighborhoods; one of these was near our home.

Takoma Park started in 1883. Benjamin F. Gilbert, an aggressive real estate developer, bought 90 acres of land here and promoted Takoma Park as "an idyllic suburban community with woods, rolling hills, fresh air, and pure springs—safely away from the pollution, noise and swamps of downtown Washington, D.C." Later he purchased another 1,000 acres. Some of Washington's finest homes were built in Takoma Park—large three-story, grand Victorian houses with gingerbread trim, fish-scale design, wood shingle siding, and ornamental tower shaped projections on the roof corners. In the early 1900s Seventh-day Adventist leaders approached Mr. Gilbert about purchasing land for their headquarters and other institutions. Mr. Gilbert and the Adventists appeared to have much in common; they both liked the idea of settling in a quiet suburban area away from city strife, but appreciated a railroad commuter line and trolleys that provided convenient access to the city. Both were against alcohol consumption and some homes had deed covenants which prohibited the consumption of alcoholic beverages in the home. This was a requirement that Mr. Gilbert, a staunch teetotaler, instituted. Sounds like the SDA/Gilbert connection was a match made in heaven.

In 1904 the Church moved their headquarters from Battle Creek, Michigan to Takoma Park. Some true believers felt Divine revelation led the church to move here but skeptics thought it was probably Mr. Gilbert's sales skills. In any event, they built a world headquarters' building, a hospital, a publishing house, and a college. Preachers, nurses, printers, and teachers couldn't afford the larger homes and often these were remodeled and divided into apartment units. Also smaller bungalows were built and some were precut wood homes that were ordered from a Sears Roebuck and Co. catalogue. A typical house was a wood frame structure and had stucco, clap board, or wood shingle siding and painted either gray or off white. Whether the house was a small bungalow or a large Victorian one, most had large yards with oak trees, azalea bushes, roses, and other flowers.

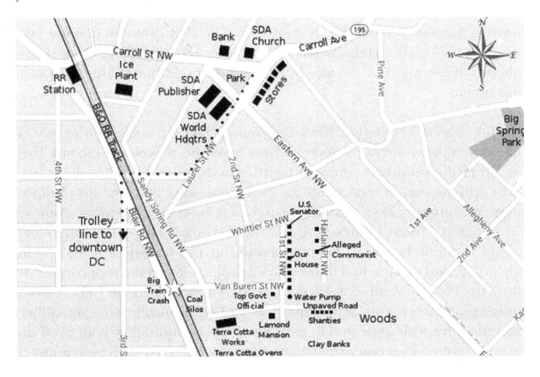

The family I first remember was my father, my mother, and an eight year older brother, Thomas, Jr. When I was six my sister Carolyn Joanne was born. We lived in one of the few brick houses in the neighborhood— a modest three-bedroom house. Our home was just two blocks from the B&O railroad line and a terra cotta works and about the same distance from small shanties where colored families lived. I use the term "colored" from time to time because it was used frequently and considered proper in the

Figure 5. Our neighborhood during the 1930s

1930s. (See Figure 5, the enlarged map of our neighborhood). In spite of railroad tracks and shanties, the neighborhood was considered a good place to live. My family was white and all the neighbors were white except for the few blacks in the nearby shanty ghetto. There may have been one Catholic couple on our street and there was one Jewish boy, Sonny Rosenblatt, in our neighborhood who kept to himself and went to a Hebrew School. In the mid-1940s the Adventist Church started a theological seminary near our neighborhood. Sonny, who was about thirteen, took Hebrew lessons there with the Christian theology students. I don't remember any Catholic kids growing up, but in the mid-forties, a large Irish-Catholic family named Doolen moved to our street.

Figure 6. Our house on First Street NW where I grew up. While this was taken in 2013 it's pretty much like it was in the 1930s. The big magnolia tree is gone.

Figure 7. I'am in front of my house with my friends Dorothy and Mary in January, 1932, about a year before my story starts.

Figure 8. My father at twenty five years old, in 1916. The photo was taken in Denver, Colorado where he taught in a business school. One course he taught was Business Penmanship.

Figure 9. My mother and older brother in about 1925, three years before I was born. She would have been thirty years old. I couldn't find any pictures of me with her. Let's see— no pictures of me with my mother, and my dad left me at the grocery store when I was a baby. In spite of these messages I feel my parents loved me.

Figure 10. Father, Mother, and baby sister about 1936.

While our neighborhood was WASP, my elementary school drew students from the row-house neighborhoods that were somewhat closer to downtown D.C. In my sixth grade class there were students with names like: Stanley Goldberg, Elaine Greenbaum, and Joe Capone—Jews and Italians not welcomed at local beaches. I was unaware of and indifferent to their ethnicity or religion, but was aware many were darker complexioned than I was, and I even envied the Mediterranean types who got a rich tan in the summer. I turned pink. When I was thirteen, I was invited to several great birthday parties of my buddies, but had no clue the parties had something to do with religion.

The New Deal attracted many workers to D.C. in the 1930s and the Adventist church had moved to Takoma Park earlier. Consequently our neighborhood consisted of largely government workers, small business people, Adventist church officials, and church publishing house workers. A couple of PhD agricultural economists lived near us and worked on controversial programs of Henry Wallace, the Secretary of Agriculture. In the 1930s the housewives didn't work outside the home, but a few unmarried women worked as secretaries. Although nationwide the country was in the middle of a devastating depression, our neighbors and most whites in D.C. had steady work, but some new arrivals couldn't find work here and became panhandlers. Almost every day, white men selling pencils and other trivial items came knocking at our door.

Washington was referred to as a "tale of two cities" during the depression: a white city with a low unemployment rate and a black one with an unemployment rate four or five times higher. Black government workers were porters, messengers, and chauffeurs, and in the private sector blacks worked as dishwashers, bellhops, janitors, domestics, and garbage men. Seventy percent of the population of Washington was white and the schools, housing, parks, hospitals, churches, and most other services were racially segregated. But unlike the Deep South, where strong segregation laws were legally enforced, in D.C. segregation was more of a tradition plus white businesses and institutions choosing not to serve blacks.

My father worked for the U. S. Coast Guard as a civilian accountant and auditor. Eventually I think he held a fairly upper level management position in the supply unit. He would sometimes talk or write in bureaucratic speak, using phrases like, "performing official Coast Guard duties at national headquarters."

But unlike our PhD agricultural economist neighbors, my father seldom carried the government issue big brown leather brief case. Recently, in perusing his papers, I discovered he had won several distinguished or outstanding service awards. In the late 1920s, before I was born, my father moonlighted as a bouncer at a night club in downtown D.C. Kate Smith, who later became a national radio and TV singing star, sang in the club where my father worked. In 1931 she recorded and performed on the radio the popular hit of the day, *That's Why Darkies Were Born.*[1] A big woman with a strong voice, she sang:

> Someone had to pick cotton,
>
> Someone had to pick corn,
>
> Someone had to slave and be able to sing,
>
> That's why darkies were born.

Ironically, Paul Robeson, the black baritone singer, civil rights worker, and communist sympathizer, also recorded the song.

NORTH TO DOWNTOWN TAKOMA PARK AND THE CHURCH

Let's look beyond our street in different directions starting with the North. As we left our house, we first pass our next door neighbor's house which was the biggest if not the best house on the block. The Petersons moved here in the early 1930s. He was a PhD agricultural economist. The house had been previously owned by a prominent judge. Three doors further to our north lived a U.S. Senator, Mr. Frazier, a Republican from North Dakota. He was active in agricultural issues. I was sometimes invited into his home, along with other children, to play with his Scotty dog. He and his wife were just regular people to us. We had no idea he was such a "big shot." After he left the Senate in 1943 and moved away, the large green mail collection box on the corner near his house was removed by the post office.

---

[1] By Lew Brown and Ray Henderson © 1931 (Renewed) Chappell & Co. Inc. (ASCAP) and Ray Henderson Music Co. Inc. (ASCAP) All Rights Reserved.

Neighborhood residents no longer could drop off their letters and small packages in the box, but had to take them a mile away to the local post office. Mary, my friend next door, and I would often put old newspapers and other trash in the collection box and then try to be at the box when the mailman came to open it to see his reaction.

The Senator's house was the last one on First Street—the street came to a dead-end here. To continue north to reach downtown Takoma Park, you had to take either a jog to the left and walk along second street or turn to the right and walk along Eastern Avenue. Either way, in two or three more blocks you came to the Takoma Park town center, the last trolley stop from downtown D.C. Here was the Piggly Wiggly grocery, the Park Pharmacy, a

Figure 11. Our next door neighbor's house where my friend Mary Peterson lived. It was the largest house on our block. This was taken in 2013 but the house looked substantially the same in the 1930s.

couple of banks, a shoe repair shop, a Ford dealership, a Chinese laundry, a hardware store, a bakery, a café, and a few other small businesses. The Seventh-day Adventist (SDA) World Headquarters, publishing house, and church were here. The Adventist Hospital and college were about another mile northeast of the town center.

We purchased all our groceries at the Piggly Wiggly store and often had shoes repaired at the shoe shop rather buy than a new pair. The shoe shop was run by a swarthy Italian with a heavy accent. I was conscious he was different, but I never heard any negative comments about him. In 1935 we bought our first car at the Ford dealership. My mother attended the Adventist church irregularly, but she wanted her children to go regularly. One late December my mother had to take my father to the Adventist hospital emergency room because he had come home from work deathly sick and acting strangely. The diagnosis—inebriation. My father had over indulged at the office Christmas party, and my mother was humiliated because alcohol use was an anathema for Adventists.

We didn't patronize the Chinese laundry. Instead, the Toleman laundry truck from a company that served the entire D.C. area, sometimes picked up our laundry at our door. I was only vaguely aware of Asian people, but other kids and I chanted:

Chinky, chinky Chinaman sitting on a fence.
Trying to make a dollar out of fifteen cents.

I recently confessed to my grand daughter-in-law, who is of Chinese and Japanese decent, and mother of my great grandson, how we chanted this naughty verse as children. She responded, "Nothing wrong with that, sounds like a good description to me." She was raised in Hawaii where teasing, mostly good natured, about ethnicity, including one's own, is a state past time.

When I was a baby my father wheeled me in a baby buggy to the Piggly Wiggly to shop. He left me alone in the buggy inside the store while he picked up a few items. While shopping, he ran into a neighbor lady who lived across the street from us. She asked my dad if he wanted a ride home in her new car. It was probably a Model-A Ford. He gathered his groceries and rode home with her. At home he remembered—oops, he forgot me! He ran all the way back to the store.

When I was only four or five I used to walk to the Takoma Park center with the next door neighbor girl, Mary, to buy penny candy at the café. We were close friends and played "Doctor" next to the coal bin in Mary's basement. The cafe had a candy case near the cash register at the front of the store. Long strips of black licorice were my favorite. The street car conductors and motormen came here for coffee, and I remember the waitress, a

Figure 12. The home of our neighbor, U.S. Senator Frazier. Not only was it a fine home for the times, but he probably also maintained a residence in North Dakota. While this was taken in 2013, it looked the same in the 1930s except there was a mail collection box near the fire hydrant.

middle aged, plump woman who always wore a dirty apron. The cafe was filled with a blue haze—almost everyone was smoking.

In 1933 my father took me to the Citizens Bank with some gold coins which would soon be no longer legal to own because the country was going off the gold standard. The bank opened an account for me with the gold coins and gave me a little steel bank in the shape of a barrel for saving money. I kept this account for more than twenty years, but closed it when the bank refused to cash a credit union check. Banks hated credit unions because they are not-for-profit financial institutions owned by the depositors and are able to pay more interest on savings and charge less interest on loans than commercial banks.

One Friday evening I was attending a young people's meeting at the Takoma Park Adventist Church. I was sitting in the back under the balcony with Donnie Rapp. We were both about fourteen or fifteen years old. Taking out a paper and pencil he whispered, "I want to draw you a beautiful mountain scene." (Attention readers. You may want to draw the scene yourself by following the detailed directions that come next before reading the rest of the story, or you can skip the next paragraph and find out how Donnie's picture turned out. But do not let your young children draw this picture.)

He drew an upside down "V" about 2 inches wide and 2 ½ inches high to represent the mountain. "The mountain is snowcapped," he continued, and drew a line about ¾ inches down from the peak of the mountain to represent the bottom of the snow cap. But he used a little artistic flair in making this line and drew it as a small cursive "w" (no sharp angles, just graceful curved ones) but one side of the "w" was a little lower than the other. He said, "The sun is shining over the mountain." He drew a circle about a ¼ inch in diameter. The center of the circle was about ½ inch above the mountain peak. He added about ¼ inch long lines around the circle's circumference to represent the sun's rays. Finally he said, "There is a big cloud over the mountain." He drew a large upside down "U" about 2 ½ inches wide and 4 inches high. It was centered over the center of the mountain and encompassed the mountain and the sun. The base of the upside down "U" was near the base of the mountain. He was finished with drawing.

"Oops, what's this? It's my old man bending over the toilet," he said. I got the picture. The sun represented a body part "where the sun don't shine." The snowcap represented the family jewel package. Donnie's "old man" was the Church's pastor. Wow! This was a holy man of God ordained to preach the gospel bending over the toilet.

One other Church event happened when I was maybe eighteen years old. One evening a visiting Pastor, Elder Rebok, was preaching the service. He was president of the Adventist Seminary where Sonny Rosenblatt studied Hebrew. Toward the end of the meeting he started talking about how wonderful it was that so many people had been members so long and given so much service to the church. "Has anyone here been an Adventist church member for more than seventy years?" he asked. Maybe five or six raised their hands. "Wonderful! Would you dear saints please come forward and stand near either wall?" They did. He repeated the sequence: sixty years, fifty years, forty years, etc. When he got to twenty years or so he worked in five-year increments and finally one-year increments. I stood near the wall when he got to five years. Finally everyone in the church was standing up near a wall or the front of the church except for a handful that had never joined the church. Then he pressured them (he would have said invited them), to give their hearts to God and come forward and join the church. No one did. The eyes of about hundred and fifty church members standing around the perimeter of the sanctuary were on six or seven people remaining in the pews. The minister tried harder. "These are the last days, Jesus is coming soon, you must not wait another day, come forward and join us," he beseeched them. Still the obstinate sinners held their ground. At the time I thought, "Something's not right here," and I admired those who did not budge. Reflecting back, I think the service was cruel trickery. This, however, was not the typical way the Adventist church won new members. Samir Selmanovic, a writer and pastor, wrote, "Organized religion is like anything else in this world, beautiful and broken…" While this meeting was broken, the Church has engaged in many noble works.

Carolyn Votaw, the sister of President Warren G. Harding who died in 1923, lived a few blocks from the church. In the mid-1920s, probably after President Harding's death, my parents lived in a small second floor apartment in a house next door to Mrs. Votaw and her husband. My parents and the Votaws became close friends, even though the Votaws were considerably older than my parents; they had a role in converting my mother to the SDA church. Carolyn's husband, Heber, was an Adventist minister and important church official but served as Director of Federal Prisons during the Harding administration. Yes, I was named for Heber Votaw and my younger sister for Carolyn Votaw. I was never happy about having an unusual name. Only a few times in my life did anyone say, "I am pleased to meet you, Heber." It was rather, "How do you pronounce that again?" or "What kind of name is that?" At least my parents didn't name me Doris like a man I recently met, the son-in-law of a neighbor. Doris introduced himself with a smile and said, "Yes, my parents named me Doris," and went on to tell some funny anecdote on why. I've recently learned about another man, who was a junior that pronounced his name the same way but spelled it Dorris. I should have been more proactive in explaining my name and relaxed when introduced to people. Maybe it was OK for my mother to give me an unusual name since hers was Epsie. She was named after her half-brother's wife who was part Native American.

Sometimes I felt resentful and wondered if my parents named my sister and me after the Votaws just to ingratiate themselves with their semi-rich and semi-famous neighbors. Looking through the lens of more maturity, I believe my parents sincerely respected the Votaws. My mother particularly admired Mrs. Votaw, a well-dressed, stately, impeccably mannered role model. My parents never mentioned the Votaw's wealth or their relationship to a U.S. president. I was a teenager before I even knew that Mrs. Votaw was the late President Harding's sister. Our family received only small gifts from the Votaws. When my sister was about two, they gave her a fine blue velvet dress. For a few years they gave me religious books for Christmas, which I never read. When I was twelve or thirteen they gave me a book, with several chapters on the birds and bees, called *On Becoming a Man* by Harold Shryock, M.D. He was professor of anatomy at the Adventist medical school in Loma Linda, California, and many Adventist boys were exposed to his book which warned of self pleasurement dangers, such as a lag in mental development. Dr. Shryock recommended avoiding "highly spiced food and food consisting principally of animal proteins" to reduce stimulating the reproductive organs, but I'm currently waiting for this stimulating diet to start working.

The Votaw house wasn't anything grand, but was a little above average for a Takoma Park home. It was well furnished and had many memorabilia from Burma, such as carved ivory elephants; they had served as missionaries there. I admired Mrs. Votaw's fine Chrysler sedan. It had two jump seats in the back and held eight people including the chauffeur, and we were frequently chauffeured around town in it on pleasure tours. Elder Votaw had only a small coupe and no chauffeur. In the late thirties, the Votaws built a lovely redbrick, three story home with large white columns in front, near the Adventist hospital and college, built with money inherited from the Harding estate. It was and still is one of the finest homes in Takoma Park. The house had an elevator, and my sister and Elder Votaw got trapped in it when he was showing off the amenities of his new house. On their death, the Votaws left the house to the Adventist College, where it has served as a residence for the college president. The college is now a university.

North of the Takoma Park town center was the unincorporated community of Silver Spring, MD, and beyond that dairy farms and woodlands. There was heavy clay rich soil here that was ideal for pastures. Contented black and white Holstein cows grazed the grasses, and in the fall one saw fields with shocks of wheat or corn.

EAST TO THE BIG SPRING PARK

About five blocks to the east of our house was a natural spring—often referred to as the Big Spring. People came here with gallon glass jugs and filled them with cool natural pure water untreated with chlorine or other chemicals. The spring was in a small park with a dilapidated hexagonal bandstand and a playground. My father walked with me to this park on Saturday afternoons after he got home from work. Then Federal employees worked five and a half days a week. He never joined the Adventist church and didn't rest on the seventh-day Sabbath.

While I played on the swings or went down the sliding board, he read the *Evening Star,* one of D.C.'s major newspapers. Even as young as five or six I liked to look at the political cartoons by Clifford Berryman on the front page of the *Star.* I didn't understand most of them—just liked to look at the funny pictures. I had a difficult time with the tall skinny guy with a long white beard, top hat, and striped pants. My father told me his name was Uncle Sam. I had a great uncle named Sam, but he didn't look or dress like the fellow in the cartoons. My father said, "Uncle Sam is an imaginary figure who represents the United States of America." I didn't understand an "imaginary figure" and how he represented an entire country.

One time when we were at the spring, the Weller Brothers were there using the playground equipment. They were in my Sabbath School class—same idea as Sunday school in mainline Protestant churches. While I played on the swings, my father as usual was reading the *Evening Star.* One of the brothers asked, "Your father doesn't read the newspaper on the Sabbath, does he?" The other one said, "I can't believe your father reads the paper on the Sabbath." Many of the more orthodox Adventists didn't read secular material on the Sabbath. I was surprised the Weller boys talked so religiously since they were rather naughty at church. Also I was not entirely sure Adventists should swing and see-saw on the Sabbath, but I didn't know reading the newspaper on the Sabbath was bad. I was embarrassed and hurt that they thought my father was so bad. I knew my father was a good man and a gentle man. When he was in his nineties, if a woman walked into the room, he would get out of his chair and offer her a seat. He had fortitude. One time he was having severe abdominal pain and took a city bus to the hospital where his appendix was removed. Back to the newspaper issue, I mumbled some kind of incoherent response to the Weller boys' questions. The next Saturday my father said, "Come on, Heber, let's go to the spring." "I really don't want to go today." I replied. That was the end of our walks to the spring. Years later the Health Department found the spring was polluted and closed it down.

The orthodox position of no newspaper reading on the Sabbath may be extreme, but one might find it rewarding to set aside one day a week to focus on spiritual things rather than the secular and material. According to the Bible, Jesus said, "The Sabbath is made for man, not man for the

Sabbath." Could one find this gift by using the Sabbath to read and contemplate on higher ethical issues of life, such as, the beauty of nature, how to help others, and how to cope with life and face death? Although ninety-five percent of Christians observe Sunday as the Sabbath, perhaps it's OK to observe another day that has an older tradition and, some would say, based on a sounder scriptural position. While one may face hardships in trying to observe Saturday as the Sabbath, such as missed job opportunities, there could be strength in following your own quest and not the crowd. One doesn't have to be a believer to be a Sabbath keeper. There are such things as atheist Sabbath keepers just as there are kosher atheists. It can just be a family tradition. As youngster I was only interested in playing and didn't look forward to a day of contemplating spiritual matters.

Going further east there were truck farms and orchards. Farmers sold their fruits and vegetables at roadside stands. After my parents bought a 1935 Ford, I often rode with my mother out to these stands where she bought fresh local produce. Driving further east, especially traveling southeast, one drove past tobacco fields and tobacco barns that reminded me of western Kentucky where my uncle lived. About thirty miles east of our house we would reach the Chesapeake Bay, with the beaches that didn't welcome Jews or Italians. If you crossed the Chesapeake Bay by ferry, you reached the eastern shore of Maryland. This is where my college friend Carl was born. He told me, "We were so poor that I was lucky to be born a boy because otherwise I wouldn't have had anything to play with."

SOUTH PAST THE SHANTIES TO THE U.S. CAPITOL

Walking about a half block south from our house and crossing the street, one reached a house rented by the Alves family. The family moved to D.C. from Texas in about 1940. He was a top official in what is now the Department of Education. My sister became a good friend of Ann Beth, the younger daughter. It was during the early years of the Truman Administration that Mr. (or more likely 'Dr.') Alves and his wife were invited to a White House dinner. I was about seventeen and active in photography and they had me take their picture before they left for the evening. She was dressed in a long evening grown and he in a tuxedo. A few years later their older daughter, Mary Virginia, married Horace Busby a Texas political activists. In the late forties, Busby became a speech writer and advisor to Senator Lyndon Johnson and held the same position when LBJ became president. Busby was considered by many to be LBJ's best speech writer. My sister met Mr. Busby several times and said he was very outgoing and pleasant.

Jack Rollins lived with his parents across the street from Alveses with his parents. When I was grown I heard that he was gay. In the 1930s I really didn't know much about gays. A neighbor came across him in downtown D.C., and Jack was dressed as a woman. As a youngster, about the only thing I heard about Jack was "he's a little different."

In this paradise of Protestant whites, "happily situated... among majestic oaks," was a serious blight. Our street, First Street, ended about another half block south from the Alves and Rollins homes. At the end of our street were woods, a large clay field, and terra cotta works. If you turned left here and walked a short distance down a hill on a dirt road, you would reach five or six shanties where colored people lived. These shanties had no electricity, running water, or indoor plumbing. Many of the children were crippled with rickets because they didn't have milk to drink. Few attended school past the fourth grade.

If, on the other hand, you turned to your right, you would see a three-story old Victorian house. The Lamond family, owner of the clay banks and terra cotta works, at one time lived here. The people from the shanties probably settled here years earlier to work in the clay fields, when clay was dug with pick and shovel and put on carts. The men still sometimes worked at the terra cotta plant or a nearby fuel company and the women as domestics in the white homes.

Why in the 1930s in a segregated city would a city planning agency or neighbors tolerate a colored shanty community near the home of a U.S. Senator, a top government official's home, and a fine Victorian mansion? The answer is that it was a southern tradition. Just as on the southern plantations where the owner often provided housing for slaves and sharecroppers near the big house, the terra cotta owners provided housing on the terra cotta property for the colored workers. There was a similar colored settlement on the Maryland side of Takoma Park. In the 1930s "colored" was the polite term to use for blacks. It was near Maple Avenue where the city parked the garbage and trash trucks, and the men in this shanty community probably worked as trash and garbage men. There was still another shanty ghetto about three miles north of the city limits in what is now Wheaton. There were several of these small colored communities that ringed the city near other terra cotta works and other industries.

Figure 13. A little black shanty on Call Place in Southeast Washington, D.C. There were a number of black shanty communities around the outskirts of D.C. (Courtesy D.C. Public Library, Washingtoniana Division)

Just past the shanties was the clay field—a deep gorge cut into the side of a large hill formed from years of mining clay. The gorge was two or three city blocks in area and ten or fifteen feet deep in some locations. The gorge was like a giant irregularly shaped bowl with finger-like cuts reaching out into the hillside. The topsoil and other non-clay material had been scraped away and piled up in mounds around the perimeter of the field leaving gray, blue, and red clay exposed on the sides and floor of the gorge. It was an unreal landscape and a great place to fool around, build roads and castles, run, jump, explore, and play hide and seek. At the highest point of the clay field you could look south and on a clear day see the Washington monument.

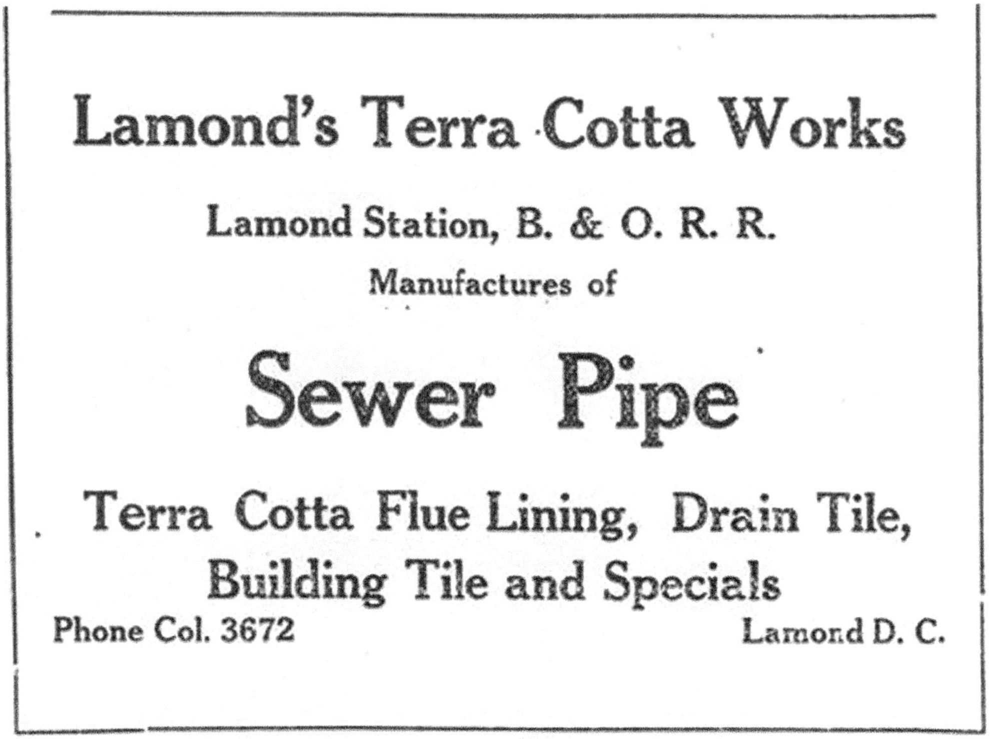

Lamond's Terra Cotta Works

Lamond Station, B. & O. R. R.

Manufactures of

Sewer Pipe

Terra Cotta Flue Lining, Drain Tile, Building Tile and Specials

Phone Col. 3672   Lamond D. C.

Near the clay banks was a large three story red building, where workers ground and blended the clay with water—the terra cotta works. This building was filled with conveyors, bucket elevators, and all sorts of neat

---

Figure 14. An advertisement for the Terra Cotta works near our house (Source, Dorothy Barnes)

machinery. Near this building were four or five beehive kilns where they baked the clay products. My friends and I could look in through the small doors and see the glowing fires in these ovens. While I never saw bricks at this plant, I saw rows and rows of orange-red large diameter drain pipes and hollow clay tile building blocks. There was something calming about warm oven fires and warm earth colored terra cotta products. Between the clay fields, the mixing plant, and the ovens, we had excellent, but somewhat dangerous, places to play. Once in a while we saw one or two black men who worked around the plant, but no one chased us away. For the most part the terra cotta works seemed to operate on its own, without human beings. By the mid-thirties the plant was dying. Cinder blocks were replacing terra cotta building blocks and steel and concrete pipes replacing clay pipes.

Figure 15. Remains of a terra cotta kiln on the grounds of the National Arboretum. This kiln is somewhat larger than the ones near our house.

At one time Washington was a major brick producing center of the nation. In much of the city's subsoil was found the finest clay for making bricks and other terra cotta products. Further down the railroad tracks from our house, near what today is the Fort Totten Metro station, there were thirteen acres of clay mines and brick manufacturing. It was called Terra Cotta, D.C. My guess is there was a shanty ghetto of blacks here also. In the 1930s there were probably ten or more small terra cottas or brick plants just within the city limits.

My older brother and I often walked south on the railroad tracks to go downtown. The U.S. Capitol was about six miles due south of our house. We passed Terra Cotta, D.C., and went through the community of Brookland, the home of Catholic University. Finally we reached Union Station, and the nearby U.S. Capitol. We would just walk into the Capitol building. In the mid-1930s there was little security, and often there wasn't even a guard at the desk at the entrance door. We roamed the building freely because this was the people's building; the government couldn't keep them out. We climbed the winding steep metal stairs to the dome and looked out over the city. We walked hallways with signs that said, "Members Only." If it was a weekday and Congress was in session, we entered the House or Senate gallery. Most of the time we saw Congressmen or Senators reading newspapers or walking around greeting each other. We rode the subway from the Russell Senate Office Building to the Capitol. The Capitol was our playground. To us it was just a big white building, and we didn't really appreciate its majesty.

We visited other government buildings. There was an aquarium in the basement of the Department of Commerce building and a small museum in the Federal Reserve building. Most of the time there was a guard stationed at the door, but often he was away. When he was on duty at his post he usually ignored us because he was busy working a crossword puzzle. The nation's capital was blissfully unafraid of terrorist attacks.

A second or third cousin of mine, Gene Dulaney from Murray, Kentucky, visited us in 1940. In his early twenties, he was interested in politics, and took me to the Capitol to meet his congressman. We met with Nobel Gregory in the House Office Building, where he treated us most graciously. He talked to Gene like they were the best of friends, mostly small talk about Murray, not much about politics. Then he led us on a tour of the House Office Building and the Capitol, including the congressional gymnasium, the cafeteria, and the visitors' galleries in both the House and Senate chambers. We even stopped to pee in the restroom reserved for congressmen. When we entered the Senate gallery, Senator Rush Holt from West Virginia had just started speaking. He began in a slow quiet tone, but soon he was ranting in a loud voice against the 1940 Selective Service Act which called for our country's first peace time draft. When he finished, many in the gallery clapped and cheered, including my cousin, even though demonstrations like this were forbidden. In the days that followed, Senator Holt's speech received much publicity. This was a big event, but I was only twelve and the whole thing didn't mean anything to me. I don't know if Gene was ever drafted into military service, but he studied law and eventually became known as a "hanging" judge in Lubbock, Texas. I doubt he ever actually sentenced anyone to be hung, but he was proud of his reputation of handing out harsh sentences. Congressman Gregory continued serving until he lost the democratic primary in 1958. Senator Holt lost in the 1940 democratic primary, but continued campaigning against any U.S. involvement in the war until his antiwar campaign abruptly ended with Pearl Harbor.

The U.S. Capitol and other nearby grand marble federal buildings hid terrible squalor of crowded colored housing. In the two large black ghettos in downtown D.C., people lived in rundown brick row houses or apartment buildings, but I believe these people probably had a better life than the people of the shanty ghettos in the suburbs. Many inner-city colored had better services than the suburban shanty ghetto people, who had no electricity or running water, although as many as ten percent of inner-city ghetto dwellers had no electricity or running water. Those in the suburbs had little or no access to medical care. To my knowledge neither the Adventist hospital in Takoma Park, nor the Catholic hospital near Brookland, nor the Methodist hospital in upscale Palisades Heights admitted colored. Freedman's hospital, located in downtown D.C., was established during the Civil War to meet the needs of African Americans. It was one of the few places colored could get medical care.

In 1952 my wife, Dolores, was working as a nurse in the Adventist hospital in Takoma Park. A black man came to the emergency room with serious chest pains. The hospital did not admit blacks and called Freedman's Hospital to try to send him there. Freedman's staff refused and told the Adventist hospital, "You must treat him there." The Adventist hospital staff put him by himself in a large room that normally held two patients. It was probably at least another five years before the Adventist hospital or the other hospitals were integrated.

My brother and I never visited the downtown ghettos, but now reflecting back, I believe we would have been safe there. When I was around twelve years old, about 1940, I took piano accordion lessons after school at Kitts Music Store in downtown D.C. I rode the city bus, and in the winter I returned home after dark. Before WWII, D.C. was a peaceful and safe southern city. My greatest musical achievement was playing Brahms' *Hungarian Dance No. 5 in G Minor*. A brutally frank friend said, "Your timing is terrible." I hope I didn't disturb the peace of Mr. Brahms' soul. A Far Side cartoon around the 1990s showed angels in heaven giving out harps to new arrivals and the devils in hell giving out accordions.

Once in the mid-1930s my father took me to a parade on Pennsylvania Ave. It was Labor Day, Memorial Day, or some other major holiday. I saw marching bands from the Navy and Army, Boy Scout troops, and Shriners—the whole works. Near the middle of the parade a group of people marching in close formation approached, dressed in white robes and wearing white pointed hats. Some wore face masks. About one-third of the spectators cheered and applauded. I asked my father, "Who are these people?" He gave a vague answer. At least he didn't applaud. I was almost grown before I knew what the KKK was all about. In the late 1940s, I met for the first time, my uncle Robert in Texas who was one of my mother's older brothers and a successful veterinarian. For some reason the subject of the KKK came up and he said, "When I was young I was a member of the KKK, and I never had so much fun in all my life, riding around on horseback at night in my white robe scaring darkies." Ironically, Uncle Robert supported Lyndon Johnson's run for the U. S. Senate in 1948, and when Johnson became President he successfully promoted civil rights legislation. Maybe both Uncle Robert and LBJ matured.

WEST TO THE RAILROAD TRACKS AND INDUSTRIAL PLANTS

The B & O railroad tracks were a couple of blocks from our house and ran from Union station, about six miles south of our house, north-west to Chicago. Several industrial plants were located along the side of the tracks. In addition to the Lamond Terra Cotta Works, there were the large coal silos of the John Meiklejohn fuel company which sold fuel oil and wood in addition to the coal. Most homes were heated by coal, and fuel oil was just coming into vogue. When I was nine or ten I had to shovel coal into the furnace as well as help my father carry out the furnace ashes to the alley behind our house, where they were collected by the ash man. We also had a trash man and a garbage man. All were colored. When I was five or six a really big and really black man in gray coveralls came to pick up our garbage. He had a gentle look and I asked him, "What do you do with all this garbage?" With no hesitation he re-plied, "Wes makes chewin gum outa it."

To the northwest of us near the railroad track was an ice plant. Most homes had ice boxes rather than refrigerators. At this plant they made ice and delivered it to homes two or three times a week. We ran behind the ice truck to pick up ice chips, ice from the large blocks the ice man had to chop into smaller blocks. It was so clear and the best tasting ice ever.

My friend, the late Stewart Bainum, bought the abandoned ice plant building in the late 1940s. He hitchhiked to the Washington area in 1938 from Ohio when he was almost penniless. His father had worked at the Ford plant in Detroit but lost his job and went to work on a WPA project on the Blue Ridge Parkway. His grandfather helped support the family by ped-dling fruits and vegetables from a horse-drawn wagon. Stewart worked as a plumbers' helper in the D.C. area and eventually bought the ice plant with no money down and converted part of it to a plumbing shop and rented out the rest to a building insulator. The rent from the insulator helped make the payments on the building. This started Stewart on the road to becoming a very successful businessman and philanthropist. He and his family eventu-ally became the majority shareholders of Choice Hotels International Inc., a leading worldwide hotel franchisor.

Across the railroad tracks from the ice plant was the Takoma Park train station. Workers from the ice plant used the restrooms at the station since there were none in the plant. At one time as many as 15 commuter trains a day stopped at this station, but by the 1930s only one train every few weeks stopped here. Hobos riding into town on freight trains often got off the train near Takoma Park, and I would often see them camping out at the clay banks or in the nearby woods.

The railroad tracks and steam trains were an important part of my life. By day I played on the tracks and watched the trains go by. At night I laid in bed and listened to the comforting sounds of the steam train engines. My three-year-old niece who lived with us for a while didn't find the trains so comforting. She was terrified of them, but eventually got used to them. In the summers our family rode one of these trains on the first leg of our trip to visit relatives in western Kentucky, a favorite place for me. I always wanted to hop a freight train like the hobos and take a little ride but never got up the nerve. When my Takoma Park friend Harold was about sixteen and walking near the train tracks, he wanted to go to Silver Spring, three or four miles away, and decided to hop a freight train. Soon one approached creeping toward Silver Spring. He jumped on the ladder of one of the cars and thought, "This is great." But soon the train was picking up speed and he was afraid to stay on and scared to jump off. Soon he did jump. He hit the ground hard and rolled over a few times but with no serious injury. "It was one of the dumbest things I ever did," he told me recently. Harold's family had moved to the D.C. area from near Scranton, Pennsylvania, in the mid-1930s to find work. Harold said they were tired of eating cornmeal mush twice a day.

In the early 1940s, when I was about twelve years old, I was coming home from school one sunny afternoon. To reach home I had to go through a viaduct that went under the railroad tracks. A major surprise awaited me at the tracks. The engine and coal car of a freight train had rolled off the track and were lying on a steep bank. They had crashed into another train. The engineer who had jumped from the train was killed when the engine rolled over on him. The police wouldn't let me pass through the viaduct and I had to go through another one further up the line. Both my sister and I were late getting home and my mother was frantic.

Let's continue our trip westward. On the far side of the railroad tracks, about three quarters of a mile from our home, was the Walter Reed Army Medical center. This was another place my father took me on walks when I was five or six. It was a most attractive place with rose gardens, fountains, ponds and beautiful old red brick buildings, but no swings or sliding boards. There were two large iron gates at the entrance that were always open, and I can't remember ever seeing a sentry there. If one was there he never questioned us. We just walked in. Now the entrance is equipped with concrete barricades and two or three heavily armed guards. The medical center is now at a new location in Bethesda, Maryland.

It was the first and last time I went to any church with my father. It was a small wood frame church, not far from Walter Reed where a non-denominational fundamentalist congregation met. They called it a tabernacle. The pastor was Dr. Clark J. Forcey. One of his five children, also named Clark, was my classmate in the third or fourth grade. Like Donnie Rapp, the preacher's kid who drew naughty pictures of his Dad, Clark was naughty. His conversation was chockfull of profanity and obscenities, and he told lots of dirty stories. He was the best marble shooter in the class and played for keeps, meaning he kept all his opponent's marbles which he shot out of a circle we had drawn in the dirt. I lost many marbles to Clark.

My aunt Bertie, my mother's older sister, started worshiping at the tabernacle, and she praised Dr. Forcey's preaching and told my father he must go hear him. He finally went. Did he go because he thought he might hear a really good message or just to get his sister-in-law off his back? I have no idea, but my guess is it was the latter. One evening, probably a Sunday evening, he took me to a revival meeting at the tabernacle. Why he didn't take my mother or any other family member, I don't know. Other than funerals or weddings, this is the only time I remember my father attending church. This lack of church attendance is ironic, since I have seen letters of references for my father when he was a young man, and they described him as a dedicated Christian. We sat near the back of the church at the end of a row. There were mostly adults in the congregation; I was one of the few youngsters. There was hymn singing and preaching, and then they got to the real business—an altar call. While the congregation sang, "*Jesus Is Tenderly Calling Today,*" the preacher, who must have been Dr. Forcey, called for people to come forward and surrender their hearts to God. An altar call can be a very gut wrenching experience if one takes it too seriously. If you don't go forward, you will spend eternity in hell, burning in the lake of fire. On the other hand, the idea of surrendering your will has an aspect of defeat. What if God directs me to become a missionary to an African leprosy colony and I don't want to? Plus you may question, "Why should I obey this preacher who reminds me of a used car salesman?" In this meeting, I didn't take the call seriously because I was only about ten years old and felt this meeting was for grown-ups. This particular preacher didn't look like a used car salesman. In any event the preacher kept pleading for people to come forward, and four or five deacons worked the crowd, by encouraging people to go forward. My father turned to me and said, "Let's get out of here." We left. Pastor Forcey died in 1940 at the age of thirty nine. But his memories live on, in the large fine Forcey Memorial church building (aka the Forcey Bible Church) in Silver Spring, Maryland.

Moving further west from the tabernacle, one reached Rock Creek Park. The other side of the park was, and still is, the upscale part of the city and mostly white. Still further west the city limits stop at the Potomac River.

LITTLE WHITE TRASH BOY ENCOUNTERS BLACK PEOPLE OF THE SHANTY GHETTO

THE ONLY WAY OUT

There was only one easy way out of the little shanty settlement near our home— only one way for the residents to get to stores, schools, or the trolley line which provided access to churches, friends, and relatives, and that way was down our street. The other sides of the settlement were surrounded by woods, clay fields, railroad tracks, or a tough white neighborhood.

Usually it was only the children who came out. They never walked alone, but rather huddled together in a group of three to six. These kids didn't hop, skip, run, laugh, bounce balls, shout, or poke each other. As they entered our block they cautiously looked to see where the mean dogs and white people were. I think they were deciding what side of the street to walk to avoid these threats. After choosing the less threatening side, they moved forward silently, almost slinking along, trying not to be noticed. Some shuffled by in oversize shoes. Those crippled with rickets limped along awkwardly. Almost every day we saw kids on their way to school or to the store. My school was about a half a mile away—theirs almost two miles away. However, their school attendance was sporadic. When they shopped at the stores, they returned with only a small brown bag containing perhaps a loaf of bread.

The children were dressed in ragged clothes that didn't fit, like urchins in a Charles Dickens' story. In the summer they were barefoot. In the winter they might wear shoes that were too large and had no shoe laces, and in the coldest weather they only had light sweaters or jackets. They had no umbrel-las, rain coats, or boots. If we walked close to them, we thought they had a certain odor that was unique to colored people. To what extent the odor was real or imaginary, I am not sure. After all they didn't have running water in their homes for bathing or laundering.

They didn't smile, laugh, frown or cry. They carried a kind of blank, sullen or depressed look. I had also seen terror on their faces when neighborhood dogs ran out barking and jumping. The neighbors would call off their dogs, but not with a lot of firmness, like maybe it's ok to scare these black kids a little. My high school friend, Margaret, who lived near the shanty ghetto on the Maryland side of Takoma Park, told me she and her brothers would let their dog run out and frighten the black children who passed their house. It seems like scaring little black kids was a form of white entertainment.

When we passed the children on the sidewalk, there were no greetings or eye contact. They would drop their glances toward the ground, and we pretended we didn't even see them. We ignored them; they avoided us. It was almost a denial on the part of whites that this shanty ghetto was there or that these people even existed. It was a cold indifference.

At Easter and other special Sundays, some of the colored ladies dressed in dark dresses and white hats, and walked by on their way to catch the trolley to church. Perhaps they were on their way to hear Elder Lightfoot Gordon Michaux, a popular black preacher of the time. He had a Sunday morning radio program where he preached and shouted, or some would say raved, nonstop without any pauses. But he had an upbeat message, "Happy am I with my Redeemer." We often tuned on his program, but probably more for entertainment than for spiritual guidance. For the people of the ghetto living in squalor and pain, his message of hope must have been im-portant. However, it is doubtful that many of them had radios to listen to it.

I would also see women who worked as domestics walking along our street, but I don't remember ever seeing an adult colored male on our street. One of my brother's friends who lived across the street from us once saw a colored man walking towards the ghetto carrying a terrapin by the neck. This was probably the families' evening meal. It suggests that hunting and gathering were a significant part of their food supply. They probably trapped rabbits and squirrels and gathered wild blackberries and hickory nuts.

For the most part neighbors hardly ever mentioned these people. Adults didn't refer to the people of the ghetto in a derogatory manner. They didn't call them niggers, but rather Negroes, darkies, or colored. One time I used the N-word and Mother quickly chastened me and said, "You must use the word 'colored;' that is what they like to be called." I think she was not only concerned that I had used an offensive term but also that I had used slang. She was strict on using correct English. I might say, "Mother, can I go out to play?" Permission wasn't granted until I said, "Mother, may I go out to play?" I seldom heard any unkind racist words from family or neighbors. One negative remark I heard was when my mother was talking to Mrs. Barkhausen, a neighbor lady, on the sidewalk and some colored children walked by with their school books. This woman said, "It's a shame the government wastes its money on trying to educate these people." My mother just shrugged her shoulders. She thought education was the solution and not the problem. She was actually rather enlightened for the times. However, sometimes when I left my room cluttered she would say, "This place looks like a Negro shanty." Other than this, I never heard my mother or father make any disparaging remarks about people's race or religion.

On the other hand, no one expressed a concern about the injustice and squalor. The Adventists were concerned about warning the people of the Second Coming of Jesus. The PhD agricultural economists were concerned about crabgrass in their lawns. The Citizen's Association debated how to best beautify the neighborhood. The people of the ghetto lived on in their world of squalor; we lived in our middle class world. That's just the way the cards were dealt. However, my mother, from time to time, did give some of our old clothes to a woman who worked as a domestic in our house.

One day I broke the unspoken rule of ignoring the colored as they walked down our street. I was perhaps seven or eight years old when two or three colored kids came down our street, walking across the street from our house. They were about my age or even a little older. I was standing near the safety of my house and could have easily run in to Mother if there was a problem. I yelled out, "Black clouds." I don't know why I did it. I hadn't heard this expression. I imagined the news flash would read:

> *Brave lone white lad challenges pack of older colored rowdy hoodlums.*

To my surprise, they yelled back, "white trash." I had never even heard them talk before and wasn't sure they could. "What is this 'white trash' stuff?" I thought. I didn't like being called trash. I felt, "It's not fair. That's worse than what I called them." Of course, I had to run in to tell Mother what these bad people called me. I thought she would straighten this out by going to see their parents. "What does 'white trash' mean?" I asked. She said, "Don't worry about it; you just leave those children alone." She must have known they wouldn't have initiated the exchange of insults. For years these four words: "black clouds" and "white trash," were the only exchange I had with these children. In a sense, insulting them was less rude than ignoring them. At least you recognized them as human beings. Another news bulletin:

> *Seven year old delicate white child scarred for life when called "white trash" by gang of insensitive black rowdies.*

About three years later I had another encounter with the children of the ghetto. I was about ten years old and playing with some toy soldiers and trucks at the clay banks with one of my buddies. There, at the edge of the woods were three or four colored kids. They moved cautiously closer, then stopped, looked us over, and moved closer still. We kept them under surveillance trying to read any sign of hostility. "Were we going to have a show down?" I asked myself. No, they just wanted to see our toys. We talked and played together a little while and then they left. That was the last and only real encounter I had with these children. Yet another news bulletin:

> *Noble ten year old white youth takes giant step for better race relations.*

I did have an encounter with some black kids in Rock Creek Park a couple of years later. It was about 1940 and the National Park Service had just opened the park to black people. I was there with one of my buddies and my parents, having a picnic. After lunch my friend and I took off down one of the trails and soon encountered a group of five of six black kids. One was our age and the others younger. This encounter was not so amicable. They more or less challenged us. I called the boy our age "Rochester," the name of Jack Benny's black butler on his comedy show. The boy took a swing at me and soon we were at it in full force. My friend and the other black children stayed out of it. There was a sense of fair play on both sides. It more or less ended in a draw but my friend and I retreated back to my parents and I didn't mention the incident to them. I'd been told to leave these children alone years earlier. Major new flash:

> *White youth, previously cited for noble race relations work, found guilty of making racial slur and nearly causing a race riot in Rock Creek Park. Park Service reviewing wisdom of its desegregation policy.*

A Dark Stranger in the House

She was big, and had a blue-black fat face with broad homely features, thick lips, and short unkempt hair. Her eyes appeared dull, the whites a little blood shot. She wore a simple dark blue tattered housedress, old black shoes with badly worn heels, and no stockings. When she wore stockings, they were rolled down to the ankles. Her name was Myrtle. She worked in our home as a domestic one day a week and came from the shanty ghetto near us. She was about thirty years old.

Our family frequently employed colored domestics during the mid 1930s and early 1940s when I was between six and twelve years old. Mother paid them the going rate, a dollar per day. While Myrtle walked to our house, other domestics came from one of the big ghettos near downtown Washington and had to ride the trolley. The big issue was whether the housewife should pay the domestic an extra 20 cents for trolley fare. Mother thought it was the domestic's responsibility to get to work, and she didn't want to pay car fare, but usually wound up paying the extra 20 cents or at least compromised on an extra 10 cents. Before paying, however, she would check with the neighbors, "Do you pay your girl's trolley fare?" And the housewives would go into a big discussion of the equity of paying car fare and other problems they were having with their domestics: not showing up for work, stealing things, or being just plain lazy. Others would brag, "My girl is simply wonderful."

To Mother, Myrtle was one of those wonderful girls. While she didn't work fast, she worked hard and steady: dusting, vacuuming, mopping, washing clothes, ironing, and whatever else Mother told her to do. She never took a break, was completely trustworthy and seldom spoke a word. When she did speak, she mumbled in low almost inaudible words. I remember her down on her hands and knees scrubbing our green linoleum kitchen floor. When I entered the kitchen a huge rear end faced me with the dress hiked up exposing big black bare legs.

I didn't like her and I knew she didn't like me. On the box of pancake flour, I had seen the face of a smiling happy colored lady. In the movies, the cheerful colored maids, dressed with clean white aprons and hair tied with a neat kerchief, frolicked with Shirley Temple and the other white children. Or when the white children were distressed, the understanding maid would comfort them by pulling the child to her warm large bosom. Myrtle wasn't cheerful or comforting. When she came, a black cloud moved in over our house. It was like the preacher said, "For behold the darkness shall cover the earth, and gross darkness the people." It seemed as if the sun stopped shining, the electric lights were turned low, and the shades partially drawn. In all the time she was in our house, I don't remember exchanging any words with her. I would carefully pass her in the upstairs hall, and we didn't even look at each other. Once in a while she would give me a side glance, that I felt was filled with contempt. She was probably thinking, "Dis little spoiled, white trash boy make me sick. Him fussen about his milk not cold enough, his coat ain't a right color, and him don't has enough toys. Our chillens ain't evens got no milk, warm coats, or toys." News flash:

> *Mean black domestic puts evil eye on innocent self- sacrificing white child who is saving his pennies to send missionaries to save the souls of African children.*

I would have loved nothing better than to have told on Myrtle and to have gotten her fired. It would, however, have taken more than a mean look to Mother's little precious to get her fired. After all, Myrtle was one of those "wonderful girls." As I reflect back, she may not have been mean at all, but rather shy and uncomfortable talking to anyone white, even a little boy. And she may have been a little retarded, perhaps because of inadequate nutrition.

Myrtle kept moving in and out of our lives. She would work for several months and then suddenly disappear. I didn't know what happened to her. Did we let her go because we couldn't afford her? Maybe she had found full time work or became pregnant. These issues were not something my parents talked about in front of us children. In any event, Myrtle would return in two to six months to work again for awhile.

SEARCH FOR MYRTLE

One day my mother said, "Go tell Myrtle to come this Thursday instead of Wednesday." I questioned this task. "How will I find her? What house does she live in? What's her address, her last name?" Mother said, "Just go, you'll find her." When Mother commanded, I obeyed. (Mother talked, looked, and acted like a younger Miss Daisy in the movie, <u>Driving Miss Daisy.</u>) I was only eight years old and wore thick glasses that kept sliding down my nose. Mother would give me a sign to push up my glasses. She would make a little upward stroking motion at the top of her nose. And if I happened to be standing around with my mouth open, there was another sign for this problem. Mother would tap the bottom of her chin with an upward stroke. On top of all this, in summer I wore kind of sissy short pants. My skin was whiter than white with a tint of pink, despite being in the sun all summer.

I was afraid to go to the colored settlement alone. Here, the people weren't just tan, they were black. I had once walked down the road that ran by the settlement with my older brother, but I'd never gone alone. However, many times I stood at the top of the hill where the road led to the settlement and saw the shanties in the distance and wondered about their world so different from mine. The idea of social injustice never entered my mind. This was just the way things were.

Further down the road past the shanties, the road ended at Eastern Avenue, unpaved at that time. People called this area "Hell's Bottom." Here, poor whites lived who had a reputation for being tough. I felt the older boys would like nothing better than beating up a little sissy kid from the better neighborhood.

Mother gave me a little push out the front door. I walked past the magnolia tree in our front yard—a reminder of our southern heritage, and walked south on our street, past our neighbors' houses all painted and well maintained. The lawns were green, the hedges neatly trimmed. The yards were filled with hollyhocks, roses, and day lilies. I walked for about a block and a half until the street ended in woods. Here was the gravel road that led to the colored settlement and beyond the woods were the clay banks.

At the entrance to the gravel road was a green water hydrant where the blacks came for all their water. The cylindrical hydrant was about three feet high and six inches in diameter. This was the type of hydrant they had at many playgrounds in the city. We just had to push a button on top and a strong stream of cool water gushed forth from a spigot on the side. I stopped and got a drink. I was stalling, afraid to move down a strange road.

Finally, I got up my nerve and turned to walk down the narrow one lane gravel road. I had seen a car go down this road only once or twice. The road descended at a moderate grade and ahead I could see the shanties. I thought, "What am I going to do? Which house do I go to? Will they know Myrtle?" While there were only five or six houses in this community, it seemed like a big neighborhood to me, and I could imagine someone in this community not knowing the neighbors by their first names. After all, I didn't know the first names of most of our neighbors. They were all Mr. or Mrs. to me.

I reached the first house and like the others, it was an unpainted wood shanty with only one room. The floor was about two feet or so off the ground.

Wide, vertical gray weathered boards covered the sides of the house. Narrow vertical boards covered the cracks between the wider boards. The houses had simple steep gabled roofs and most of them had a front porch. The houses were spaced about twenty feet apart. Just walking by, I could look through the front door all the way through the house and out the back door. I saw only an unmade bed, a couple of chairs, a table with a kerosene lamp, and a stove. My mother had used a poor analogy comparing my cluttered room to a Negro shanty. I had toy soldiers, games, books, shoes and shirts scattered around my room. The little shacks were almost bare of toys or clothes. About the only clothes they had were on their backs. And there were no lawns, hedges or flowers, only dirt yards.

Figure 16. Interior of a black shanty in Washington, D.C. The shanties near our house looked much like this except they were one room and one could see all the way from the front through to the back door. (Courtesy D.C. Public Library, Washingtoniana Division)

It must have been a Monday morning. There were black cast iron kettles of water heating over open wood fires in the yards and the women were washing clothes. White sheets were draped across a line between two large oak trees. I was fully acquainted with washing clothes in cast iron kettles. I had seen my aunts, in rural Kentucky, use the same method.

The children were playing, many of them limping, crippled with rickets. I thought, "Maybe these are the kids I called 'black clouds' when they walked past my house. Will they get revenge? Will their parents stop them from beating me up?" A few black men in bib overalls with no shirts were just standing around. No one looked my way or talked. It was like they didn't see me. "Was I invisible or only a spirit or ghost or maybe they were the ghostly aberrations and not me?" It was like a silent movie. I didn't see Myrtle anywhere. "Who should I ask? What if they didn't speak my language?" The trees seemed higher, thicker, and darker than normal. The shanties were drab and dreary and the people indifferent, wearing ragged clothes. I was afraid. I imagined Mother would be reading the following news flash:

> *White eight year old sissy boy with thick glasses boiled in cast iron laundry kettle by savage Africans. City fathers unaware of tribe's existence in Washington. City is outraged at mother for sending this precious little child on such a dangerous mission.*

But I had an even greater and more realistic fear. That the story would read:

> *Angry mother severely scolds sissy eight-year old boy with thick glasses for failing to carry out a simple mission that a four-year-old could have handled. This rather slow, shy white boy couldn't find Myrtle, the family domestic, who lived in a small settlement of gentle and helpful colored folks just blocks from the family home.*

44

I had almost reached the last house in the settlement and hadn't seen Myrtle. I was just getting up the nerve to ask someone about her when she appeared out of nowhere. There in front of me was a very big and black barefoot woman dressed in a ragged dark blue housedress. She didn't say a word. I said, "Mother wants you to come Thursday instead of Wednesday." She nodded and left, and I hastened a quick retreat going back up the gravel road, turning right onto our street. The houses seemed bigger and brighter, the lawns greener and neater, and I felt secure again.

JOSEPHINE BRINGS LOVE

One day a new domestic came. Josephine was older, slimmer, and a lighter hue than Myrtle. She had a certain dignity, spoke English well, and was reported to have some college education. She didn't live in the nearby ghetto but rode the trolley car to our house. When she came to work the house was literally brighter. She turned on more electric lights and raised the window shades all the way up.

I would tag along as she cleaned, asking questions: why this and why that. Unlike most adults, she seemed to genuinely enjoy talking to a little kid. If Mother was out shopping, Josephine would fix me a sandwich and we would sit down at the table and eat and talk. Or if Mother was upstairs napping, Josephine would take a break and we would just talk about the big issues of life. I might take her hand and turn it over and ask. "Why do colored people have black skin but palms that are almost white?" "To give little white boys something silly to ask about," she replied. Another news bulletin:

> *Enlightened colored domestic understands little pampered white boys also need tender loving care.*

One day I overheard my mother talking with my father. "Josephine just doesn't seem to be getting her work done. I wish we could get Myrtle back." I interrupted the conversation, "Josephine works really hard," I said." No one was listening. A week or two later Josephine was gone and I never saw her again and a little later Myrtle showed up at our door for work.

3

NICE COUNTRY FOLKS LIVE WITHOUT ELECTRICITY AND GROW A DEADLY CROP

Choo Choo Train

It was 1933, the peak of the Great Depression. I was five years old. My mother, older brother, and I were boarding a train at Union Station near the U.S. Capitol in Washington, D.C. We were bound for western Kentucky, not far from the junction of the Ohio and Mississippi rivers, on our way to visit relatives on a small tobacco farm. Like ninety percent of U.S farms then, this one had no electricity. We would spend the summer here. My father, who was fortunate to have a "govment" job, stayed home to work. The massive steam engine choo chooed gently and spewed whiffs of white smoke as the mostly white passengers boarded. While the passenger cars were integrated, later when we crossed the Ohio River into Kentucky, whites and blacks were segregated.

Soon the large B&O train moved away from the station, rolling through hills of western Maryland, mountains of West Virginia, and flat farm land of Ohio on its way to Chicago, stopping in a small Indiana town where we caught an Illinois Central train bound for New Orleans. It was scheduled to stop in Paducah, KY, where my uncle would meet us. It was an overnight trip to Kentucky and we were taking a Pullman car. In the evening we went to the dining car for supper, and mother complained about the high prices. Later, a black porter dressed in a clean white coat and a black cap, made up our beds. Unlike the men at the shanty ghetto back home, he was polite and friendly. The bed was so clean and comfortable and the gentle rocking of the train soon put me to sleep, feeling safe with my mother next to me.

The next day the train crossed the Ohio River and arrived in Louisville, Kentucky. We had entered the South or at least the almost-South. Kentucky was a border state during the Civil War. The train maneuvered a lot—switching and adding cars here. Kentucky law, or maybe just tradition, required that the trains be segregated. All this effort was to get probably less than a dozen black people in a car away from whites. A few hours later we arrived in Paducah, where my uncle Marvin and one of his sisters were waiting for us on the station platform. See the two maps showing the location of the Kentucky family farm—the first, Figure 17, showing the whole state and the second, Figure 18, a more detailed map of just western Kentucky. The latter map is a current map of the area except the Purchase Parkway that runs through the middle of the area is not shown. Many of the roads shown on the map were here in the early 1930s but many were not paved. The lakes on the eastern side of the map were created by the TVA in the late 1930s.

Figure 17. Location of the Kentucky family farm.

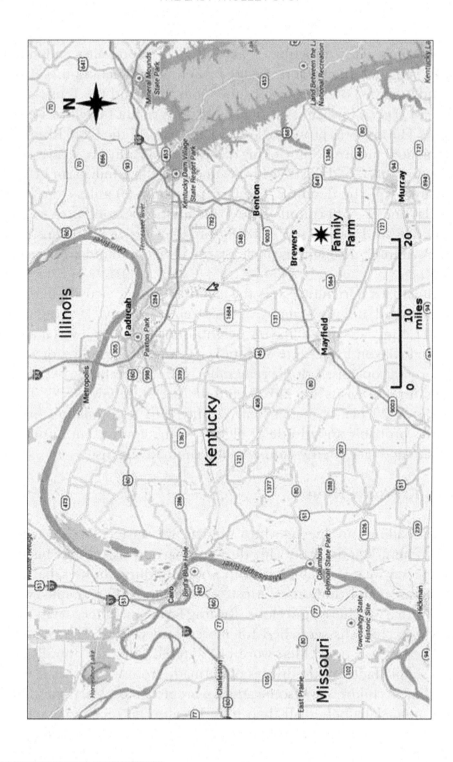

Figure 18. Detailed map of western Kentucky.

Kentucky is often thought of as a state of mountains and hillbillies. Paducah is part of the western wedge of Kentucky touching the Mississippi River and bounded on the north by the Ohio River and the Tennessee River on the east. This is low land. My uncle said, "We're not hillbillies, we're gully jumpers." The area was prone to flooding and in 1937 the Ohio River flooded and devastated the area. Some of my relatives from Paducah, a fairly large city on the Ohio River, had to stay with my uncle on the family farm in Marshall County to escape the flooding. The farm was about 30 miles from Paducah. Marshall is one of eight counties that made up the Jackson Purchase, an area purchased by Andrew Jackson in 1818 from the Chickasaw Indians. Down at the creek running through my uncle's farm, we often found arrowheads.

In the 1930s agriculture was the main economic activity here. There was widespread unemployment and extreme poverty. Demographically, Marshall County was much like my neighborhood in D.C. It was made up of white Anglo-Saxon Protestants with only a few Jews, Catholics, or Southern or Eastern Europeans. I don't remember seeing one black person in the county during my visits as a kid. Even today there are few blacks. The 2010 census listed 49 blacks in Marshall County with a population of 30,000. There was probably an attitude of bigotry in the county, but in the thirties there were no blacks in the county to discriminate against.

My Old Kentucky Home

After loading our luggage into the car, we started for the farm near Brewers where Marvin lived with three unmarried sisters and his mother. Along the way we saw small farms with wood buildings: houses, barns, cribs, smoke houses, and outhouses. Most of them, including homes, were un-painted with a weathered gray look. Rusting farm machinery sat in the front yards where chickens scratched for insects and worms. The people were poor. The soil was poor. Men wore old tattered blue bib overalls and the women simple faded housedresses often made from feed sacks. It was sum-mer and most children and some adults wore no shoes. Marvin and his fam-ily were financially better off than most because he received a small WWI pension, there were four able-bodied workers in the family, and no young mouths to feed. He drove a big car—a black 1931 Chrysler sedan which had the boxy look of a Model-A Ford but was bigger and more luxurious. Many families didn't own a car; they rode to the store or church in a mule-drawn simple farm work wagon—the same wagon used for hauling corn, hay or tobacco. Uncle Marvin often dressed in nice slacks and a shirt rather than rough bib overalls. On hot summer days when going to town he wore a solid cylindrical flat top stiff straw hat with a two or three inch wide brim that was popular in the 20s and 30s—the type of hat worn by barbershop quartets.

As we came nearer the family home, the paved U.S. highway turned from blacktop to gravel. A large cloud of orange brownish dust from the gravel trailed behind the car as we drove. Stones spun off the tires and struck the under bed of the car with noisy blows. We passed through Brewers, a community of about 20 homes, a high school, a Methodist church, a general store with a post office, an auto repair shop, and a doctor's office. Dr. Bean, M.D. had a large attractive white clapboard house surrounded by a low black wrought iron fence. His office was here with shelves containing rows and

Figure 19. Mules were the major power source in the rural south in the 1930s. (Source, Library of Congress)

rows of colorful medicine bottles and pill boxes. He was middle aged, a little plump, sang in the church choir, and was a church leader.

In 1948 the Brewers High School boys' basketball team won the Kentucky High School championship. When I visited here in the mid-1940s when I was about sixteen, people asked me, "Do you play ball?" They didn't use the word basketball around Brewers, they just said ball.

It was a mile from Brewers where we turned on to the one lane dirt road that would take us home and another a half mile along this road to the house. Woods and fields on each side of the lane made a picturesque drive. We forded two small streams to reach the house. Reflecting back on this road I think of John Denver's song about West Virginia country roads that took him home to the place he belonged.

This wasn't West Virginia; it was Kentucky, but this road was taking me to the place I belonged. This drive gave me a lasting love for this country road and country roads in general. Later in life I served on the Rural Rustic Roads Advisory Committee for Montgomery County, Maryland.

We soon turned off the country lane and drove up a small incline on a dirt driveway to the house located on a seventy five acre farm. The farm was more or less divided into thirds. The front third included the farmstead with the house, barn, corn crib, garage, smoke house, chicken house, pig pen, and outhouse. There was a small fruit orchard and vegetable garden, as well as a pasture for the cows and mules, and a field for cultivated crops, usually tobacco. When I was twelve my uncle taught me to drive a car in the cow pasture. At this time he owned a green 1936 Chrysler sedan. I had to sit on a pillow to see out the windshield. After I learned to drive in the pasture, we took the car out and drove on the state highway. I asked my uncle, "What if the State Police see me driving?" He said, "Don't worry about it." In the four or five years I drove under age we never saw a police patrol car.

The next third of the farm was woodlands of oak, hickory, and sweet gum trees. It was too steep for planting crops. Uncle Marvin taught me how to make a tooth brush from a sweet Gum tree. He took out his faithful pocket knife, cut off a six or eight inch twig, and peeled an inch or so of bark off one end of the twig. Where the bark was peeled off he split and spread the exposed soft fibrous core into bristles. *Et voilà,* a toothbrush.

When I was ten or eleven my father took me squirrel hunting in these woods. He carried a twenty-two rifle and I scouted for squirrels. We hadn't been hunting for long when my father got a sudden call from nature and needed to do number two. He went behind a large oak tree and dropped his trousers. About the same time there was a rustling in a nearby treetop "It's a squirrel," I whispered. Father stumbled from behind the tree with his trousers down around his ankles, trying to pull them up and aim the rifle at the same time. It was painful to see my father in such a humiliating position but the scene wasn't as bad as the picture Donnie Rapp drew in the Takoma Park church of his father. We returned to the house without any squirrel or my father's pride.

The last third was the bottom lowland with a creek running through it. My uncle and I spent a lot of time there looking for arrowheads, and he taught me how to skip rocks over the water. He would pick up a flat rock and with a sidearm pitch, skim the rock two or three hops over the creek bed pools of water. This bottom land was usually in corn or tobacco. A tobacco barn was there and what remained of a four room log cabin where my father and his siblings were raised. Most of the fields on the farm were surrounded by split-rail fences. Once, one of my aunts was stranded for several hours on the far side of the creek and couldn't return home. When she was working in one of the fields, a sudden heavy rain erupted and quickly filled the creek with rushing water.

On the neighboring farm was a shanty where a sharecropper lived. The really poor were the sharecroppers—farmers who owned no land or houses. They lived in shanties on someone else's farm and raised tobacco or corn on the owner's land. The crops they raised were shared with the owner who received about one third of the harvest. Once I visited this share-cropper's home to play with the children. Their little shanty reminded me of the shanties in the black ghetto near our home in D.C. The one-room house, covered with the gray weathered wood, was about twenty by twenty feet and was about two feet off the ground. It had a simple gable roof which extended over a small front porch. There was little furniture. Most of the family of five slept on pallets, small cloth mats, on the floor. The lives of these white sharecroppers appeared much the same as those of the blacks that lived near us in D.C., but there was a difference. People showed these sharecroppers some respect, though the dire poverty of both was treated with indifference.

In contrast, Marvin and his family lived in a large painted white bungalow. A large porch surrounded the house on two sides. The wood-shingled roof of the main part of the house extended over the porch. In summer daylight hours the porch was the family's living room, with straight-back cane chairs, a large rocking chair for Grandma, a porch swing, and pallets on the floor to lie on. The home had three large bedrooms, a living room, a dining room, a large kitchen, a large hallway with a bed, and a small workroom with a cream separator and buckets of well water, with a metal dipper for drinking and shallow enamel bowls for washing your hands and face. All the family plus visiting neighbors would drink from the same dipper, but Mother didn't allow me to

.Figure 20. An abandoned farmhouse in Calloway County Kentucky probably once occupied by a sharecropper. This drab house resembles the shacks in the ghettos near our home in D.C. (Source: Murray State University, Special Collections and Archives, City of Murray and Calloway County Collection)

drink from it. I had to use a clean glass and a fresh water source. There were no bathrooms, running water, electricity, or central heating in the house. There was a small water closet in the living room. It had a small seat with a hole and a slop jar below the seat. This was grandma's private bathroom. My aunts used the two-seater outhouse in the woods near the house. My uncle just used the woods. There was a bed in the corner of the living room where Grandma slept. When she went to bed early, the family continued conversing in normal voices. She couldn't hear anyway.

Figure 21. The family Kentucky farm house as seen from the country road.

The floors, baseboards, doors, and all the house trim were dark oak. The walls were covered with flower-patterned wallpaper or with plain wood paneling and windows were covered with neatly ironed white curtains. Beds were covered with beautiful quilts handmade by my aunts. The house exuded a warm, clean, comfortable feeling.

The attic was the most interesting place in the house, used mostly for storage. The ceiling was the underside of a gable roof with exposed rafters. The roof ridge ran along the middle of the attic where a tall adult could easily stand up. But where the ceiling sloped to the edge of the attic, I would have to crouch down to see what was in the corners. Twists of dried tobacco hung from the rafters. Old issues of the *Saturday Evening Post, Country Gentleman,* and old newspapers lay in neat stacks. There were hand tools, various gadgets, discarded dresses, and men's suits— lots for a young boy to explore.

My uncle's and father's WWI khaki uniforms complete with helmets and gas masks were stored in a box in the attic. The pants were knee length with cloth leggings that wrapped around the legs below the knees. I would try to dress up in one of them, but of course they were way too big. My uncle and father had both served in France—Marvin was a motor pool mechanic, and my father a stretcher bearer in a medical unit on the front lines during the Meuse-Argonne offensive, one of the bloodies battles in U.S. history. My father never said much about the war. He did say the trenches were very muddy, a foreign looking soldier stole his coat, and a loaded stretcher was really heavy. When it was too much to bear you yelled to your partner, "stretcher down."

At home he sometimes said, *"Vamoose tout suite,"* to tell us, "Get out of here now" or "Let's go right away." He learned this in France, and I assumed they were French words. Recently I learned it's a combination of English slang, *"vamoose"* used by WWI doughboys meaning, "to depart quickly" and the French words, *"tout suite"* meaning, "right away." "Vamoose, derived from the Spanish *"vamos,"* means "let's go." Americans picked this up in the southwest during the mid-1800s. So it is a redundant expression and literally means something like, "Let's go right now, right away." In any event this is a good expression to use when you want to tell someone it's time to go. Just say the magic words, *"Vamoose tout suite."*

Like Marvin, father received a small pension for a partial war disability. The story I remember was that he had been gassed, most likely by mustard gas. Mustard gas, which causes blisters in the respiratory tract, had been used in several battles near the end of the war. While my father died of respiratory problems, he was almost one hundred years old and I question if he was ever gassed. Rather, the government was probably very liberal in giving out small pensions to veterans.

Uncle Marvin was in his late forties and a small man—maybe five feet, six inches. He was very self-conscious about his height and would say, "I'm only a runt." My father was almost six feet tall. But Marvin was a skilled craftsman and could make or repair almost anything. His youngest sister, my aunt Ethel, was outgoing and the friendliest of the aunts. The middle sister was Alice, the quiet one and the best looking. The oldest sister was my aunt Molly. She was the tall-est and considered the wisest and most well-read, but her hands were twisted and her fingers curled up with arthritis. The three sisters, all in their fifties, were often referred to as the "Girls." My grandmother was thin, toothless, and had to gum her food. She had broken her hip a year earlier and walked with crutches the rest of her life. She was hard of hearing so it was difficult to talk with her, and she just sat in her rocking chair at the edge of the porch, chewing tobacco and spitting the juice out over the porch. My grandfather had died years earlier in an accident involving a mule. He not only farmed but sold Bibles and served as an itinerant Methodist preacher. Why Uncle Marvin or his sisters weren't married I didn't know. I heard stories about my aunts' earlier boyfriends and learned years later that Aunt Alice, the pretty one, had once been married for a short time.

Figure 22. My father's mother and siblings in front of the Kentucky home in the early 1930s, about the time I first remember visiting here. Standing from left to right: Molly, Alice, Lee, Ethel, and Marvin. Julia Ann, my grandmother, is seated in front. Lee was a half-brother who lived in Paducah, Kentucky.

None of the family had more than a sixth or eighth grade education, but they all spoke proper English. However, from time to time, they dropped in some hayseed expressions like, "He went down yonder." Both my mother and father went on for higher education in Bowling Green, Kentucky where they met. Mother graduated from Western Kentucky State Normal School (a school for training teachers) and my father from Bowling Green Business University. I think, today, calling the business school a university would be considered an exaggeration because the courses were probably more like bookkeeping and shorthand than economic business analysis.

This family arrangement, with middle-aged single man living with his mother and three old-maid sisters (pardon the politically incorrect term), must have seemed strange to the neighbors and perhaps was the subject of gossip, but it was all normal to me. These were my favorite relatives. This was my father's family, but apparently my mother preferred staying with these in-laws rather than her own family which lived about 25 miles away.

Marvin and his family grew tobacco, corn, and hay and a few times my uncle experimented with raising cotton. There were two mules, Jack and Red, which pulled the farm wagon, the plow or a cultivator, as well as providing the power for large stationary farm machinery such as a hay bailer. Three Jersey cows provided milk, about three dozen chickens provided eggs and meat, and two hogs provided more meat. A dozen feral cats ran around the yard and a dog named Rags played in the yard and slept under the big porch.

From time to time my uncle sold timber from the woodlands which was then made into bourbon whiskey barrel staves. My aunts didn't believe the family should have any involvement with the whiskey business but my uncle overruled. The money was good. The farming practices were really not much different than those used in the 1700s. The only reason a small farm like this was close to being economically viable was the growing of tobacco, a high valued cash crop.

The family was most functional and pleasant. Marvin and his sisters often teased each other in a gentle way, but I had the sense they really cared for each other. Each had their own chores and the chores weren't easy. There was no electricity, running water, or indoor plumbing. If they needed water they drew it from the well. If they needed heat they had to build a fire in the fireplace, and to build a fire they had to cut and split the wood. Uncle Marvin was responsible for the field work— planting, cultivating, and harvesting crops — but Alice and Ethel helped in the fields. In addition to the field work Marvin slopped the hogs and took care of the mules. Ethel fed the chickens and Alice milked the cows. Molly, the oldest, only worked in the house and was responsible for preparing meals—no easy task.

Let's talk more about food. Molly got up early and brought in firewood for the big black cast iron stove. She started the fire and began cooking breakfast. A coffee pot was soon percolating. Before long she had eggs, oatmeal, and either bacon, ham or sausage cooking. She baked fresh biscuits that were served with gravy. There was home-made butter, fresh cream, and milk. I can't remember if I was allowed to eat the pork. I do remember eating squirrel once which of course tasted like chicken. These meats were against the Adventist dietary code, but, Mother tended to relax religious and other rules when we were away from home. I really didn't care if I had meat for breakfast because all I wanted was my store-bought cereal and milk. But I complained about the milk because it was barely cool, more like lukewarm. They tried to keep it cool by storing it in a jug down in the well water, but that really didn't work. The family ate breakfast at a long narrow table in the kitchen. After breakfast Molly kept the fire embers alive so she could heat the stove up again for the main meal at noon.

On Sundays and special occasions we ate the noon meal at a nice table in the dining room. Most of the dishes were prepared from scratch from products raised on the farm. Salt, sugar, coffee, tea, and flour were the main items bought from the store, and a few times Uncle Marvin took a sack or two of wheat to a mill to be ground into flour. A typical noon meal would consist of creamed corn, green beans, black-eyed peas, sliced tomatoes, applesauce, and cornbread. Since we were there in the summer, all the vegetables were fresh. The meat was often baked chicken. There were several jellies and fruit preserves and iced tea was the drink. For dessert we might have custard pie, peach or blackberry cobbler, or sugar cookies, and the blackberries for the cobbler were wild and picked along a fence row. After the main meal the fire in the big stove was allowed to go out. For the evening meal we went back to the kitchen and had more or less a repeat of the main noon meal except everything was served cold.

REST FROM ALL THY LABOR

On Sunday the family rested. Only the most necessary chores like cooking meals, feeding the animals, and milking the cows were done—no field work was performed. But the family did not attend church regularly. Uncle Marvin controlled church attendance because he controlled the transportation and when they did attend, they went to the Brewers Methodist Church about two miles away. The family seemed only moderately religious. They didn't say grace before meals or read the Bible. There were no religious pictures on the walls such as Jesus praying in the Garden of Gethsemane, but they did like to listen to gospel quartets on the battery-operated radio. When my Kentucky relatives attended church, the whole family went.

Religion had little part in our life at home in Washington since my father wasn't a church member and my mother wasn't a "super seven," a very orthodox Adventist. My brother's wife said my mother only went to church when she got a new hat," but I don't believe that was a fair characterization. She was religious in her own quiet way and often went to church although not on a regular basis. But my parents wanted their children to be brought up in the church. My brother and I did attended Sabbath School regularly, but my younger sister rebelled and went to the Episcopal Church with a neighbor girl and later became a nonbeliever. Growing up, I was uncomfortable being a member of a minority religion branded as "seven days grass eaters." But to be fair it was only a few times I heard anyone disparage the religion and for the most part Adventists seemed to be respected. After all they weren't Catholics or Jews. To clarify this last remark let me say I'm not really sure how much bigotry there was against the Catholic and Jews. The KKK did parade down Pennsylvania Avenue and there was the sign at the beach prohibiting Jews and Italians, but I personally heard few remarks against either Catholics or Jews. However, Adventists and many fundamentalist protestant churches in the 1930s preached that the Papacy was the Anti-Christ of Revelation and would do lots of bad stuff to God's chosen people. On the other hand, the message seemed to be that your everyday Catholic Church member was just a misguided but decent person. As far as discrimination toward Adventists, one time a physician did tell my mother not to go to Adventist doctors because they practiced quackery, but for the most part Adventist health care had a good reputation. Another factor that contributed to my discomfort with religion was being brought up in a religiously divided family. Also the fact that so many of the finest people I have known, starting with my father, were not religious has been confusing. Someone once praised my mother-in-law, one of the kindest persons I have ever known, for being religious. She responded emphatically, "I am not religious." I haven't yet resolved the big religious questions of life, but I'm working on them.

Mother and Father gave us little religious training and didn't quote the Bible or invoke God's name. There was no, "Lay me down to sleep" or any other prayers at night. The exception was once my father quoted a Bible text to admonish me. When I called my brother a "fool," my father said, "Don't ever use that word because the Bible says, 'Whoever shall say, Thou fool, shall be in danger of hell fire.'" That got my attention and I've never called anyone by that name since—perhaps idiot or stupid. One aspect of the Adventist religion which appealed to both my parents was the health message. However, my father didn't always follow the no smoking or drinking rule. Some of the message was supposedly from Devine inspiration given to Ellen White, an important church leader, and some from a secular source, the teachings of John Harvey Kellogg. Dr. Kellogg and his brother, Will, invented corn flakes. Will started the Kellogg Company and John Harvey became the medical director of the SDA operated Battle Creek Sanitarium in Michigan. There was a comedic movie in 1994 about Dr. Kellogg, "*The Road to Wellville,*" portraying him largely as a fool, (oops, bad word), but my understanding is, he was really a visionary. My brother went to high school with one of John Harvey's relatives, probably a grandson or nephew, at Forest Lake Academy, a small Adventist boarding school, near Orlando, Florida. Rather than trying to build favor with this wealthy boy from a prominent family, his classmates called him "stuck-up."

Maybe some of my parents' health practices were just fads of the time. In any event, the prevention and treatments I remember were: being taught to take little bites and to chew my food for a very long time, and being fed honey or brown sugar instead of refined white sugar. We bought five gallon tin cans of honey. Lemon pie was one of the few OK desserts. Whenever I got sick I was bathed in a hot tub of water, which seemed close to boiling, or given hot fomentations, towels soaked in hot water and applied to the infected or injured body part, and my bowels were given a heavy dose of warm soapy water. If I were sick in bed when my father came home from work, he looked in on me and said, "Did your bowels move today?" An expression I hate to this day.

Uncle Marvin would vigorously defend Christianity and the Methodist Church if there was a challenge. From time to time he would make disparaging remarks about other churches, such as the Baptists and the Christian church—meaning the specific denomination not the religion. The Christian denomination, sometimes called the Disciples of Christ or by other titles, was founded by Thomas Campbell and Barton Stone in the early 1800s in western Pennsylvania and Kentucky. They didn't play musical instruments in their churches and my uncle, like some others, referred to them by the derogatory term, Campbellites. Uncle Marvin didn't attack Jews or Catholics; there weren't any nearby to worry about. On Sunday afternoon neighbors or other relatives might come by for a visit. It was summer and they sat on the porch or out in the yard and talked.

One Sunday evening the family all went to a revival at the Mt. Carmel Methodist church about ten miles away. There were no stained-glass windows, drapes, curtains, icons, or religious pictures or decorations of any kind in the one-room church. As darkness settled over the church, the deacons lit coal oil (kerosene) lamps which sat in the windows. The glowing light was kind of eerie—with strange shadows dancing awkwardly across the walls. Protestant churches that I had seen in D.C., even the most fundamental, all had some kind of religious decorations. My guess is it was both poverty and theology that contributed to the plainness. Icons and decorations said, "Catholic."

The congregation of maybe twenty people was dressed in their finest—men in bib overalls and a fresh white shirt, women in a simple dark housedress. The preacher wore pants and a white shirt but no coat and tie. He had an altar call inviting all those who wanted to give their hearts to Jesus and join the Church to come forward. Three people did. The preacher said a few words over them and poured water on their heads from a pitcher. *Et voilà*, behold, they were now members of the Methodist church. I thought it would be more complicated than that. At least this preacher didn't use the manipulative evangelistic methods that I'd witnessed in the Takoma Park Adventist Church.

Each year on the fourth Sunday in May the family went to the Big Singing in Benton. This event lasted all day, was mostly religious music, and was held at the courthouse. Big Singing started in 1884. The music was Southern three-part harmony sung *a capella*. Shape note music was used where shapes were used as note heads to make it easier for church congregations to read the music. The notes were designated as follows:

Fa Triangle

Sol Circle

La Square

Mi Diamond

I'm not sure how do, re, and ti were handled. In the early days of the Big Singing, extra trains were scheduled for Benton to handle the thousands of people attending. People dressed in their finest, and ladies with fancy bright colored hats crowded into the courthouse's largest hearing room and hallways. The windows of the courthouse were open and overflow crowds gathered on the lawn to hear the music. This was the big rock concert of the day but with religious music.

BACK TO WORK

Monday mornings the work week started again with Alice and Ethel doing the laundry. Out in the yard they set up an improvised work table made of sawhorses and heavy planks. Several galvanized steel tubs with water were set on the table, at least one for washing and one or more for rinsing. Nearby were one or two big black cast iron kettles with water, heating over a wood fire. This looked a lot like the laundry operation I saw on my trip to the shanty ghetto in search of Myrtle. I remember one of the rinse tubs had bluing which was used to make the laundry whiter. Laundry in the galvanized tubs was rubbed on a scrub board and laundry in the cast iron kettle was stirred with a big wood paddle. The laundry was washed in home-made lye soap which was made from lard and wood ashes from the fireplace. After all the stirring, scrubbing, and rinsing, the laundry was hung out to dry on clothes lines. I can't remember how they wrung out the cloths; my guess is by their bare hands. The next day they would iron everything using heavy irons heated over a wood fire. Some of these irons weighed about twelve pounds. The "girls" must have been strong.

STORY TIME

The family all seemed to get along well together and with other people. They were the kind of folks that one enjoyed being around. However, Marvin might have minor tiffs with neighbors and business people from time to time. The sisters all had a good sense of humor and often told homey and earthy stories. Not real ha-ha stories—just stories that were told at an appropriate moment, relative to the subject at hand. For example Ethel told this one.

Two farmers were arguing over the issue of whether someone could adjust to a very unpleasant situation. (Remember how my niece got used to the noisy trains that ran near our house?) Farmer Brown said, "Yes, one can get used to an unpleasant situation; time heals all wounds." Farmer Jones said, "Not true." A few days later the two were going for a buggy ride to do some business in town. Before they got in the buggy, Farmer Brown snuck some fresh chicken manure in the sweatband of Farmer Jones' hat that was lying on the buggy seat. Farmer Jones got in the buggy and put on his hat. It was a hot day and Farmer Jones said, "What's that terrible smell?" Farmer Brown didn't say anything, just shrugged his shoulders. They drove down the country road several miles and Farmer Jones said, "I still smell something." Farmer Brown didn't comment. As they drove along Farmer Jones made fewer and fewer comments on the smell. Finally he didn't make anymore comments about it. Farmer Brown said. "Do you smell anything?" Farmer Jones said, "No, nothing." "I just proved my point," responded Farmer Brown. "Look in the sweatband of your hat."

This farm for me was almost heaven. It was a place of sweet comfort, a place where I belonged. I think most kids have a place of sweet comfort when they grow up. Maybe it's Grandma's house or a vacation cottage at the lake. The farm was a place where everything was right. I received lots of attention. It was like having not just two parents but four. While my aunt Ethel was slowly turning the crank of the cream separator she told me stories and listened to me and tried to answer my many questions, mostly about farm life. At home it seemed my parents were always busy waxing floors, cutting the lawn, or doing the laundry and didn't have time for talk. My aunts and uncle seemed more adapted at working and listening at the same time. Maybe it was the type of chores they did. My aunts and uncle were like our housekeeper, Josephine, back home. They talked to me and listened.

Devils in Paradise

This heavenly place had a few devils: horseflies, sweat bees, chiggers, and snakes. My two aunts, Alice and Ethel, were uneasy about snakes they might encounter when working in the fields. Aunt Ethel told this story about Alice's encounter with the southern black racer snake. Remember, Alice was the quiet one and didn't talk about herself. Ethel said, "One hot summer day Alice was down yonder in the bottom cornfield, hoeing weeds, and suddenly surprised a huge snake coiled up in a corn row furrow sunning itself. It was the dreaded southern black racer snake—the fastest of all snakes. It lunged at her and chased her at lightning speed. Alice dashed across corn furrows running for her life." In fact the dreaded racer is harmless although occasionally it will charge people if it is surprised or cornered, and they can grow to five feet in length. I have seen a video of the black racer snake, and they do look like they are racing in a sine wave-like pattern going thirty miles an hour. In fact, they go less than five miles an hour, about as fast as a man walking at a good clip.

I listened wide eyed and after that kept my eyes open for snakes. However, in the ten or so summers that I walked in the woods or fields, I saw only two snakes and that includes the chicken snake I describe below. Most snakes in the area were harmless but western Kentucky has been known to have copperhead and water moccasin sightings on rare occasions. One time a seven foot long black chicken snake was found slowly slithering in the driveway. Marvin, Alice, and Ethel all went after him with a shovel and hoes. I felt kind of sorry for him. While they are nonpoisonous, they will eat eggs and baby chicks.

The real devils are chiggers. They are an immature stage of mite that is so small it can't be seen by the naked eye. They live in high grass and will jump on a passerby and feed on fluid in skin cells. Once I got a really bad case of chigger bites which itched like crazy and I had to see Dr. Bean in Brewers. He gave me some orange lotion to apply which I feel was next to worthless.

No Sex Education 101

During my early visits to the farm I questioned my uncle and aunts about the farm animals. What did they eat? When and where did they sleep? How old were they? My aunts and uncle were most patient in providing answers to most questions but questions that in some way related to sex were awkward for them. If there were two pigs in a pen, I might ask, "Which one is the father and which is the mother? But male pigs are castrated when only a few weeks old. This is supposed to make them easier to handle and improve the quality of the meat. One really couldn't call this pig or that pig a father. My relatives would stumble for an answer. I might ask the same question about a pair of mules. Mules are a cross between a donkey (or in country talk, an ass or jackass) and a horse and are supposed to have the speed and intelligence of a horse and the strength and endurance of a donkey. But mules are a hybrid and sterile. So strictly speaking it would be incorrect to call one the father or mother.

Once I was out in the yard with my aunt Alice, the quiet and shy one. Chickens were scratching and pecking for insects and worms. Suddenly a big white Leghorn rooster jumped on a small Rhode Island Red hen and starting humping her. I got all disturbed and said, "That rooster is fighting that other chicken. He is going to hurt it!" My aunt hung her head and dropped her eye lids and said quietly, "Everything will be all right."

Years later when I was an early teen and knew everything there is to know about sex, I was having a discussion with my much older brother and uncle about some benign issue. I must have spoken a bad word, "prehistoric." My brother said, "There is no such thing as prehistoric." While he didn't say it directly, what he meant was there was a literal creation of the world about five thousand years ago and everything after that is history. Before that, no history. My brother had received some fundamentalist teachings in Adventist schools, and at that time I had only attended D.C. public schools where I learned a little about evolution. My uncle seemed to support my brother's position. Here was my argument supporting evolution. "Just look at the colored people (I might have actually used the N-word). Those in America are much lighter than those in Africa. They have adapted to their environment of less sunlight." My uncle was frustrated and lost for words. I figured I had won the argument, but he finally came up with an answer. I can't remember his exact words but he used the most delicate language to say, "American colored are lighter because they are the product of interracial sex between blacks and whites—namely white male masters and black women slaves." I got his message. I must have missed the school lesson teaching that human evolution took millions of years. We went in for dinner.

The theory of evolution has been a problem for the Adventist church as it has for most conservative churches. Bible genealogists, who have studied all the "begats," estimate that the earth and Adam and Eve were created about five, or at most ten, thousand years ago. How can a true believer accept evolution that teaches earth and the inhabitants thereof, started spontaneously billions of years ago with one cell life? The Adventist church has the additional problem that evolution conflicts with their key doctrine of Sabbath keeping. The church teaches that the Sabbath is a memorial of creation because the Bible says, "the heavens and earth, and all the host of them," were created in six days and "God rested the seventh day …and blessed the seventh day." For many or maybe even most Adventists, the word "days" means literal twenty-four hour days. On the other hand, evolution teaches that the earth and life on earth evolved over thousands, millions, or even billions of years with no mention of a weekly cycle with a day of rest. My late friend Peter Edgar Hare was an organic geochemist and had graduate training at UC Berkley. He was tapped by the Adventist church in the late 1950s to be a leader in its newly formed Geoscience Research Institute. The Institute was founded to support well qualified and church loyal earth scientists to study the origin of the earth. Peter fit the bill perfectly, a proven church loyalist and a smart scientist. The church paid his salary while he worked on his doctorate at Caltech. Peter told me the church was not too happy with him because after graduating he accepted much of evolutionary science, in particular, its position on the age of the earth. However, he remained committed to the Sabbath, but he was never fully able to reconcile the literal twenty- four- hour day creation story and evolution. The conflict between science and Scripture on the earth's origin was a personal conflict for Peter because he loved his church, his father had been an Adventist minister, and yet he felt he must maintain his scientific integrity. The church was probably relieved when Peter resigned from their Geoscience Research Institute to do research for the Geophysical Lab of the Carnegie Institute for Science.

It was clear the family did not like Aunt Grace. She was the second wife of Lee Bouland, a half brother of Marvin, my father, and the girls. Lee's mother had died in childbirth and his father later married Julia Ann, the mother of Marvin, my father, and their sisters. Once when the family was talking about Grace, Marvin blurted out, "She forced him to marry her." I was about eighteen then and thought I knew all about sex. "What do you mean?" I asked. Uncle Marvin seemed reluctant to talk more about it. Finally he said, "It was the Mann Act." He gave me a half-way explanation about the details of Uncle Lee's problem which I didn't fully understand. Reflecting back I think this is the story. The Mann Act was designed to attack prostitution and to prohibit the interstate transportation of females for immoral purposes. But the law's language was ambiguous and it was often used to criminalize consensual sex involving couples crossing state lines. Lee lived in Paducah on the Ohio River. Sometime after he divorced his first wife, or perhaps it was before the divorce was finalized, he and Grace drove across the river to Illinois for a little fun. Since he had violated her, she pressured him to marry her. He resisted. She reinforced her request by threatening to use the Mann Act, and the rest is history.

I learned later that my uncle Marvin had his own early experience with sex. Once when my father was in his nineties and had lost many of his inhibitions, we were reminiscing about his family and he told me that when his brother was sixteen years old, he had sex with a recently married neighbor's wife and bragged about it to the husband. Both the wife and her husband were also about sixteen. It's a wonder the husband, who surely had access to a shotgun, didn't shoot my uncle. The problem with early teenage marriages is that it almost guarantees a life of poverty. Whether by intelligent design or evolution it seems humans have a problem—their sex drive peaks at fourteen and good judgment doesn't kick in until about twenty five.

THE CONFEDERATE SHADOW

This area of western Kentucky, the Jackson Purchase, was the most Democratic area of the state in the 1930s and had strongly supported the Confederacy during the Civil war. However, I knew there was at least one Republican in Marshall County. My grandmother said, "If the Republican Party was good enough for Abraham Lincoln, it's good enough for me."

There were three small towns within fifteen miles of the family home—Benton, Mayfield, and Murray. From time to time my uncle, one or more of my aunts, my brother and I would drive to one of these towns. Benton, the county seat of Marshall County, was the closest and the town we went to most often, especially since my uncle may have had business at the courthouse. Mayfield, the county seat of Graves County, was a little farther away but had better shopping. My mother's family lived near Murray, the county seat of Calloway County and largest of the three towns, and we would sometimes visit them. It was the home of Murray State Teachers' College. My mother's brother, Uncle DeWitt, moved from his farm into a small house near the college so his only child, Theda, could attend the school. He worked as a carpenter and a handyman to support his family and pay for her tuition. In the 1960s the state legislature was considering converting the college to a university. One of my mother's sister-in-laws, Aunt Gertie, was strongly opposed. She said, "If they make the college into a university, the school will teach 'atheanisum.' " I think she was implying atheism would be the beginning of the end of morality. Today, Murray State University has been rated a top public regional university for twenty consecutive years by *U.S. News and World Report.*

My cousin Theda became an elementary school teacher after graduating from Murray State. Terrible tragedies marked her life. Her oldest daughter, a high school senior, was killed in an auto accident and then Theda and her husband divorced. She was murdered in Kansas City, Missouri, when she was in her seventies. She was Christmas shopping for the poor in a mall in the daytime when she was attacked, robbed, and beaten to death. While many witnessed the murder, no one would come forward to identify the suspects. Police finally found the murderers from investigations of two similar robberies that same day. They were three boys—two fifteen and one sixteen.

Figure 23. One side of the Murray, Kentucky courthouse square in the late 1930s. It may have been early on a Sunday morning because there are so few people. On court day or Saturday afternoon, it would be bustling with shoppers, loafers, and such. (Source: Murray Main Street)

Like most county seats, these towns had a courthouse in the town center surrounded by a large lawn. Unemployed men, who my uncle called "loafers," lounged on the courthouse lawn, stairs, and small retaining walls. Beyond the courthouse lawns were large paved areas, maybe 80 feet wide, which served as a street and a parking lot. Across from the courthouse, on the other side of the paved area, were the stores. Model-A Fords, others cars of the 1930s, maybe a horse and buggy, a farm tractor, and a few farm wagons parked on both the store side and the courthouse side of the paved area. In at least one of the towns, people parked in a row in the middle of the paved area. Drivers parked diagonally to the curb, a novelty for me because at the time in D.C. it was mostly parallel parking. When I turned sixteen I had to take the dreaded parallel parking test to get a driver's license. Eventually, I became a real expert in parallel parking. One time an audience of diners on a restaurant outdoor patio gave me applause when I parallel parked in one swoop into a narrow space.

The courthouse square bustled with activities. The businesses on the square included grocery, hardware, shoe, clothing, and drug stores as well as one or two banks—all were providing the essentials of life. There is some similarity in the layout of a southern U.S. county seat and a Mexican town. The building considered most important is located near the geographic, commercial, and social center of town and surrounded by a large hard surface area. In the case of Mexico, it's the main cathedral circumscribed by a plaza. In U.S. county seats, the hard surface area is concrete or blacktop and filled with automobiles. The Mexican plaza is paved with brick or fine stone and filled with small flower carts and people leisurely strolling about or relaxing on benches. The courthouses don't compare with the grandeur of the Mexican cathedrals.

In two of the three towns, Murray and Mayfield, a monument to the Confederacy had a prominent place on the courthouse grounds. In 1917, The United Daughters of the Confederacy provided a sixteen foot monument for the Murray courthouse. It has a pedestal with a drinking fountain and four columns supporting a five-and- a-half-foot-high statue of Robert E. Lee. In fact, my father's half-brother Robert Lee was named after him. In Murray, 800 men had joined the Confederate Army while only 200 joined the Union Army.

My maternal grandmother, who lived near Murray, used to tell me Civil War stories when I was a teenager. During the Civil War she was a young girl growing up in western Tennessee. This was her favorite:

Figure 24. Robert E. Lee watches over the Murray Kentucky courthouse square.

My great-grandpa, her father, had been a Confederate soldier. He claimed divine intervention saved him from death from a Union cannon ball, so he was certain he was on the right side of the war. When the war ended, he returned to Tennessee and set up a blacksmith shop. Later, when Union forces demobilized, a large Union Army unit marched north through Tennessee returning home to Illinois. The unit included a marching band, wagons, horses, cannons, and endless lines of soldiers. A wagon wheel broke as the Army neared Great-Grandpa's shop. A Union officer demanded Great-Grandpa repair it. He replied, "I will, if you play "Dixie." The band tuned up their instruments and played "Dixie." My great Grandpa repaired the wagon wheel and the Army marched on.

This wasn't the first Yankee band to play Dixie. A day or two after Lee surrendered at Appomattox in April of 1865, people were celebrating the Union victory in front of the White House. Abraham Lincoln came out, gave a short talk and ended by saying, "Now let the band play Dixie."

THE MOON SHINES BRIGHT

One morning Uncle Marvin said, "Hop in the car and let's go for a ride. I have some business to take care of." After driving ten miles or so we turned into a dirt driveway and pulled up near a farmhouse. It was your typical western Kentucky farm with a modest wood farmhouse, barn, corn crib, chickens pecking around the yard, and fields of corn and tobacco. The farmer came out of the house and greeted my uncle. He looked like a typical farmer—a lean man with a heavy tan and dressed in overalls. He pretty much ignored me. Marvin and the farmer talked a few minutes and then the farmer motioned Marvin to follow him. I tagged along and we walked about a hundred feet out to a corn crib. He told us, "wait here," and went inside. Moving around some clutter and small farm equipment, he went back to a corner of the crib and reached behind some boxes to retrieve something.

He came out of the crib holding a clear glass quart mason jar. This was the kind of jar my aunts used for canning corn, beans, peaches and other fruits and vegetables. I thought the jar was filled with water. The farmer unscrewed the lid and handed the jar to my uncle who very slowly took a couple of swallows and then gave an affirmative nod, handing the jar back to the farmer. I knew from my uncle's expression this was not ordinary water. The farmer returned the jar to the crib. We went back to the house where my uncle and farmer exchanged a few more words, then climbed back into the car and returned home. On the way home no mention was made of the special water. I had no idea what this was all about, but sort of knew it was something secret and I shouldn't talk about it.

Of course today I am sure it was moonshine, the illegal clear corn liquor with high alcohol content. But even today, I'm not sure if this was a moonshiner who my uncle was doing business with or an ordinary farmer who just offered my uncle a taste of white lightning when my uncle came to discuss some unrelated matter. My guess it's the latter.

RURAL FREE DELIVERY

Uncle Marvin and I talked as we walked the gravel country road from the house to the highway to meet the mail carrier and get the mail. The road ran mostly through woods crossing several gullies. We passed a small pasture, a neighboring farm house, and an abandoned sawmill before reaching the highway, a well maintained, two lanes, gravel road. It was a Rural Free Delivery (RFD) route.

We arrived ten to fifteen minutes before the mail carrier and would sit under a tree and wait, fanning off the sweat bees and flies. My uncle, dressed in overalls and a straw hat, would either chew tobacco or roll a smoke. It wasn't long before a cloud of brownish orange dust appeared in the east and a dirty car with a small sign, "U.S. Mail" arrived. My uncle and the mail carrier exchanged a few words, the carrier handed us the mail, and in a cloud of dust drove on. The mail always included the newspaper, the *Louisville Courier Journal*. Sometimes there would be a letter from other relatives, a business letter, a small local newspaper, a magazine or a package that had been ordered from Sears and Roebuck.

Rural Free Delivery started in West Virginia in 1896. Newspaper publishers were strong supporters of it and the service spread rapidly but prior to RFD, farmers picked up their mail once or twice a week at the local post office or at the railroad station. Did this man who just delivered our mail, a successor to the brave pony express riders who struggled against snow storms and hostile Indians, understand his noble mission as "enlarger of the common life" and one who strengthens the "bond of the scattered family?" It wasn't apparent from the indifferent way he handed us the mail.

In earlier days mail carriers were appointed by their congressmen and were powerful local political figures, but by 1904 mail carriers were under Civil Service and lost their political power and the job was considered routine and mundane. But words like: "enlarger of the common life" and their faithfulness and dependability sounds like a divine calling. And while it was generally against regulations, rural mail carriers sometimes performed (and still do) important non official acts, such as checking on the sick and delivering food.

Usually my uncle didn't open the mail until later. By the time we walked back to the house, it was noon and time for dinner, the big meal of the day. After dinner, the mail was the center of attention; the family was now hungry for information. There were no phones and the battery-operated radio that sputtered with static offered little satisfaction. Occasional trips to the local country store or to Benton about eight miles away provided some contact with the outside world, but the U.S. mail was a major information source.

I would sit on the porch swing or lie on a pallet on the porch floor listening as my aunt Mollie read aloud letters from cousins in Texas and from other relatives. After reading the letters, she passed them around. You could hold a letter written by a loved one in their unique cursive style, read it, re-read it, and savor it. The personal handwriting brought the writer close to you.

Notices in the local newspaper about births, deaths, hospital admissions, and church revival meetings were read aloud and discussed. We listened intently as someone read from the *Louisville Courier Journal* about the rise of Hitler, TVA developments, FDR's agricultural programs, or activities of Kentucky politicians such as Alban Barkley or Happy Chandler. Later during the war, articles by Ernie Pyle, the folksy war correspondent, were a family favorite. Today multiple electronic sources flood us with information and much of it is received with cynicism. On this Kentucky farm, in the 30s and 40s, the modest amount of print media, most of which came by mail, inspired almost a sacred reverence. Today in most of rural America, mail is delivered to a mailbox right in front of the farm house. Farmers don't walk the gravel road to meet the messenger with the noble mission any more.

In the evening we would all sit around in the living room talking, in the glow of coal oil lamps. Grandma sat rocking, chewing tobacco, and holding a tin cup to spit in but not saying too much. Marvin had a battery-operated radio turned on. We all had to be quiet when a news program was on. Marvin said, "I like to keep posted on current events." Later in the evening, I loved going to bed and sinking down in the soft comfort of the cozy feather mattress. I fell asleep to the sounds of the katydids.

KING TOBACCO

Tobacco was king, the main cash crop of this farm and most farms in the area. It was a very labor-intensive crop requiring many hours of hand labor to prepare the soil, set out the seedling plants, weed them, pull off the suckers or small shoots, and remove the tobacco worms. On most farms all the family, including children, worked in the tobacco fields where children faced a serious risk of nicotine poisoning. It's still a problem today. After all this effort, the crop could be severely damaged by a hail storm. When the plants matured, the leaf stalks were cut, split, and hung on a large stick. The stick was then hung in a tobacco barn to cure—usually with the smoke from a slow burning fire. One late summer when I was about fourteen I helped harvest tobacco.

Almost everyone in this tobacco growing area used tobacco products; they smoked it, chewed it, or snuffed it. The users included: men, women, boys, girls, and even little toddlers. My grandmother chewed, my uncle smoked and chewed, and two of my three aunts chewed. In 2012 on national television, much ado was made of a two-year-old Indonesian boy who chain smoked. In the early 1930s I saw many toddlers smoking and some were probably as young as two years old. When I was five or six I wanted to use tobacco in the worst way—either chew it or smoke it. I would say to my mother, "Bob Atlich uses tobacco and he's only four years old. Why can't I?"

She just waved me away without a comment because my question was too ridiculous for an answer. While she hated tobacco she tolerated her in-laws' tobacco use.

Figure 25. In the rural south in the 1930s children often worked in the fields. These children are helping their father worm tobacco. Even today children work in tobacco fields and risk serious problems from nicotine poisoning. (Source, Library of Congress)

There were several tobacco products available, including store-bought cigarettes. This was the top of the line for the more well to do. Then there were cigarettes that the user rolled himself. Few women smoked; they chewed or dipped snuff. The farmer would buy a small white cloth pouch with a little yellow tie drawstring, filled with finely shredded tobacco, and white cigarette rolling paper from his local general store. If the farmer was out in the field or other locations where he didn't have a table on which to work, it took some clever delicate maneuvering with his fingers and lips to get the pouch opened and a sheet of paper out of the package, to fold the paper, pour in the tobacco, lick the glued edge of the paper, and finally roll over and seal the edges of the paper —an art form I greatly admired. Some were so skilled at rolling smokes, the cigarettes looked almost store-brought. The really poor and children often rolled their tobacco in newspaper. A few years ago I learned about Christian missionaries working in Thailand who offered free Bibles to the locals. The demand was overwhelming since the Bible paper was perfect for rolling cigarettes.

Men, women, and children chewed two different types of tobacco. One was a twist of unflavored, unprocessed tobacco just as it came from the tobacco barn. The other was processed tobacco that was ground, molded and flavored with licorice or other flavors. The problem was when one chewed tobacco, in whatever form, one had to spit out the juice. Not a very lady like or gentlemanly act. It's hard for me to imagine going out on a date with a girl who was chewing and spitting. However, while my aunt Alice chewed, I never saw her spit. She was most discrete. Finally there was snuff which was used more often by women. It was finely ground tobacco that users sniffed up their nose. Later the favored practice was to hold the snuff behind the lower lip.

Edith, a second cousin of my aunts and uncle, lived in the nearby town of Murray. They considered her an "uppity" city woman, and she considered herself more cultured than her crude country cousins. She used snuff but didn't want folks to know about it. The family story went like this. Edith would sometimes order groceries and other items, including snuff, over the phone from a local store. When she came down on her list to the snuff, the clerk on the line would ask, "What brand would you like?" Edith would reply, "Just a moment" and turn her head away from the phone mouthpiece and ask an imaginary person, "Now what brand do you want?"

Until that infamous day I had never seen my dad smoke. I learned later in life that he grew up smoking, and a neighbor told me that before I was born my dad would sit on our front porch with his feet on the railing, leaning back in his chair, enjoying a roll your own smoke. After Mother joined the Adventist church, which opposed tobacco use, she didn't allow him to smoke. He stopped smoking at home but continued to smoke at work unknown to Mother. On one of our trips to Kentucky, the whole family came. One warm summer day as I wandered around the yard, I happened to look behind the barn and was surprised to see my father and uncle smoking cigarettes. I distinctly remember the details. Instead of holding the cigarette between his index and middle finger as most smokers, he held it between his thumb and index finger. He cupped the cigarette in the palm of his hand with his fingers curled around the evil product. He tilted his head back and inhaled the smoke and then very, very slowly blew it out. I had never seen such enjoyment and contentment on his face. He ignored me, and I ran into the house and told mother, "Dad is smoking." All hell broke loose. "How could you smoke?" she screamed. "I can't believe you were smoking." I felt sorry for my dad and regretted telling on him. Several years later he gave up smoking altogether. I learned later that when he was in his 80s and living in Florida he would sometimes drop over to a neighbor's house for a fuzzy navel, a cocktail made from peach schnapps and orange juice. Mother never found out about this. Dad lived to be 100.

Smoking behind the barn was somewhat of a family tradition. Years after this incident with my father smoking, other grown relatives would sneak smokes behind the barn so my mother wouldn't see them.

Five million people worldwide die annually from tobacco use, but in the 1930s few were warned of the health hazard, especially in a major tobacco producing county such as Marshall. But the county has strongly opposed liquor and gambling and the county is still dry today. Washington, D.C. may have had its bigotry and discrimination against Blacks, but Marshall County's sin was producing a most deadly product for human consumption.

SUMMER ENDS

It was the first of September, 1933. Fun on the farm was coming to an end. Time for my older brother to go back to school and for me to start kindergarten. It was goodbye to the pigs, chickens, cows, mules, cherry preserves, sugar cookies, cool creek, woods, fields and attic memorabilia. The saddest part was saying goodbye to all the doting I received from my most caring relatives. In the years that followed, returning to school was increasingly painful. With few exceptions, the teachers seemed to be getting meaner each year. In front of the whole class one told me, "Your head is so hard I couldn't pound anything into it with a hammer." And anyone who attended Paul Jr. High school in NW Washington knew about a science teacher called "Itchy" Taylor. My brother had her eight years before I did and warned me about her. She squirmed and twitched, wore a sun visor, kept the lights off, and the shades drawn. "Itchy" mumbled under her breath and some said she was using profanity—maybe saying something like, "I can't teach these little dumb bastards anything." Despite all this, she was a reasonably good teacher because her class lectures were well organized and clear.

We packed the car and said our goodbyes. No kissing or hugging, little show of emotion—not a family tradition—but I think I saw a tear or two in Grandma's eyes. Uncle Marvin drove my mother, father, brother, and me to the Paducah train station. My father had come down by train from D.C. to spend the last couple of weeks with us. My aunts had packed us a lunch of goodies—peach preserve sandwiches, sugar cookies, and the like, all neatly wrapped in wax paper in a brown paper bag. The trip back home was the exact reverse of the trip from Washington. We drove the country one lane road to the gravel highway. We passed the weathered unpainted farmhouses with chickens roaming the front yard with the rusting farm equipment, coming finally to a smooth paved surface.

At the station we checked our luggage, said our final goodbye to my uncle and boarded the train to Chicago. The train did a lot of car switching in Louisville and integrated whites with a few blacks. We changed trains in

Indiana for one going to D.C. This was about the last time we took the train to Kentucky. My parents bought a 1935 black Ford sedan and from then on the Ford usually did the job. We also had another passenger, my new baby sister.

I took these summer trips to the farm every year until 1944 when I turned sixteen. A couple of times we reverted to the train when it was tough to get gas for the Ford during World War II. Each year we discussed the progress the TVA and REA were making in getting electricity to the farm. During the war there was a setback to distributing power for domestic use. Electricity was needed to produce aluminum for airplane fuselages as well as for uranium enrichment at Oak Ridge, Tennessee, for the Manhattan project, building the atomic bomb. Indoor plumbing, central heating, good lighting, and electric refrigeration were still anticipated aspirations, although my uncle did manage to buy a refrigerator that operated on coal oil.

When I turned sixteen, I got a federal government job and for the most part stopped going to the farm in the summer. I worked part-time after school and full time during the summers for the Reconstruction Finance Corporation (RFC), an independent government agency designed to alleviate financial problems caused by the Great Depression. It provided grants to state and local governments and loans to banks and other private businesses. During WWII it shifted to providing loans to munitions factories and plants engaged in producing synthetic rubber. My title was Clerk Typist but I never touched a typewriter at work. I was really a messenger. I took a Civil Service typing test and got a 65% grade. While 70% was passing I got a special dispensation because of the labor shortage. There was a job title called "Messenger" and blacks filled these positions. They delivered office supplies and the less important correspondence to office workers. I worked in Central Files and delivered important papers to executives. In so many words I was told the phony title was one way to keep blacks out of this job. It was said they weren't smart or responsible enough to handle these important files. It's hard to understand how a teenage white kid would be considered more responsible than a middle-aged black family man.

One day at work I decided to fulfill my lifelong dream to smoke. I wanted to experience the great pleasure that I had seen my father having when he smoked behind the barn. I bought a pack of Chesterfield cigarettes and smoked half the pack the first day. I didn't feel so well and that ended my desire for tobacco.

I now regret largely ignoring my dear relatives who did so much for me. Like most teenage boys, it was girls, earning money, and sports that were top priorities, not visiting old people. Later the important things were earning a college education, getting married, buying a house, and raising a family. But this is not unusual. How many elderly people just wait for someone to call and say, "Hi Grandma, just called to see how you are doing," or, better yet, greet you in person with a big hug and say, "So glad to see you Nanna and Pap Pap."

Figure 26. My sister and I in the front yard of the old Kentucky home. I'm about seventeen, the Great Depression has ended, and about this time I stopped visiting here on a regular basis.

4

FDR AND ALLEGED COMMUNIST PROMOTE REFORMS

A New Deal

On one of my summer visits to Kentucky in the 1930s I heard one of the men in the local general store ask, "When is Mr. Roosevelt, sitting in the White House up there in Washington, going to bring us electricity and better farm prices?" Once or twice a week I rode with Uncle Marvin to the general store in Brewers. The store had two gasoline pumps out front. You had to hand pump the gas up to a glass cylinder tank on top and then it flowed by gravity into your car. The store had a U.S. Post Office which was mainly a big cabinet in a metal cage. The cabinet was divided into many compartments holding the sorted mail. The store carried packaged and canned food items, overalls and other clothing, hammers, wrenches, and other tools, chicken feed, seed, and fertilizer. My uncle went there to "trade." He never said, "shop," and he usually did trade. He traded eggs and cream for cigarettes and food items not raised on the farm, such as salt and sugar. Now that his picky nephew was visiting he had to purchase "store-bought bread," namely soft mushy Wonder bread or "store-bought cereal," namely Kellogg's Corn Flakes. His use of the words "store-bought" was not a compliment.

About six or eight men sat around in straight-back, cane bottom wood chairs and like the men lounging around the courthouse, my uncle referred to them as "loafers," They mostly talked. From time to time they might eat some saltine crackers with American cheese and sip on a soda. I never saw any checker playing. They talked about the lack of rain, the poor tobacco crops, a neighbor diagnosed with cancer, or the poorly maintained gravel highway. Uncle Marvin mostly listened. From time to time they discussed my hometown, Washington, D.C., and FDR's new program. They talked about the Tennessee Valley Authority (TVA) and The Agricultural Adjustment Act (AAA.)

When there was a lull in the loafers' conversation my uncle asked me, "Would you like a cold drink?" These were his words for a soda or soft drink. There was a stand which held a variety of soft drinks in glass bottles and several blocks of ice. I declined a drink. Mother didn't allow them. "They're just flavored sugar water."

The loafers returned to talk about the TVA, a government corporation created in 1933 that became the country's largest provider of public power. The people it served, some of the poorest in the nation, lived in the watershed of the Tennessee River. While the watershed mainly covered Tennessee, it also covered parts of Virginia, Mississippi, Kentucky, Alabama, and Georgia. TVA's role was to provide low cost power, improve river navigation, and control flooding. A number of dams and power plants were constructed on the Tennessee and other rivers. While the TVA produced low cost power, the Rural Electrification Administration (REA) helped form cooperatives for distributing the power to rural areas. These co-ops installed the poles and strung the wires. They started bringing electricity to rural Kentucky in 1937.

The AAA, on the other hand, was responsible for improving prices for the primary farm products such as corn, cotton, and tobacco. Through a system of loans and quotas or allotments on the number of acres of crop a farmer could plant, a floor on prices was established. Other New Deal programs covered farm credit, drought relief, and crop insurance. The loafers discussed the pros and cons of both the electrification and financial programs in a civil way. After all, in this most Democratic region of Kentucky, they were probably all Democrats with the same political philosophy. On a national or even a statewide basis these programs were quite controversial. Proponents of TVA argued that private power companies were greedy, charged too much, and weren't interested in unprofitable rural electrification. Government help was needed. Opponents argued there were hidden losses with government ownership and operation and distortion in the al-location of capital. Some said it would lead to socialism.

As a kid I didn't understand or care about most of this talk, especially words like "price stabilization," but I recognized the importance of electric power. Without it I imagined one lived much like natives of the African jungle or a South American mountain village—clothes were washed with a washboard, water had to be drawn up from a well, firewood had to be split, and one pooped in the woods or in a smelly outhouse. I sort of understood the idea of the TVA:

1. The government dams up a river which creates a big lake.
2. Water flows through the dam and turns a wheel in a big machine.
3. The big machine magically creates electricity.
4. The electricity goes over wires to your farm to a pump in the well.
5. The pump pushes water up a pipe to your toilet.
6. The toilet will flush.
7. *Voilà,* no more pooping in the woods or smelly outhouse.

So even as a kid I had an admiration for the TVA. Later in life I applied unsuccessfully for a job with the TVA. In the 1940s I toured the Kentucky Dam which had a large electric generating plant and played an important role in providing electricity for western Kentucky. I was in a tour group of maybe twenty-five people, and at one point the tour guide made a stop so we could use the restrooms. There were four of them, labeled as follows: White Men, Colored Men, White Women, and Colored Women. There were two drinking fountains, one for whites and another for colored. This is the only place I have ever seen "separate but equal." I've seen plenty of "separate but not equal." Here the facilities were exactly alike. Our tour group was all white and we were waiting in line to use the white facilities. Finally one brave person went up and drank from the colored drinking fountain. Then everyone started using either restroom and both fountains.

In the 1940s I hitchhiked and rode Greyhound buses around the South. At the bus depots there were separate waiting rooms, drinking fountains, restrooms, and eating areas for whites and colored. The areas for whites were bad; areas for colored were atrocious – broken chairs, drinking fountains that didn't work, and floors that hadn't been mopped in weeks. In Jackson, Mississippi, I boarded a bus filled with about sixty percent blacks and the rest whites. The bus was almost full, with the blacks sitting in the back. There was one row between the blacks and whites where one white man sat in a window seat; the other three seats in the row were empty—the only empty seats on the bus. The bus traveled a few miles and then stopped at a gas station that also served as the local Greyhound bus stop. A middle-aged, well-dressed black lady boarded the bus and sat in the window seat in the row with the white man in the opposite window seat. The driver closed the door and drove about a half mile down the highway and then he suddenly jammed on the brakes. He marched back to the woman and yelled at her to go to the back of the bus. She had to squeeze into the bench seat, all the way in the back, which was already full. I had grown up accepting the way blacks had to live and were treated because this was just the way things were, but for the first time in my life I thought, "This is not right!"

Let's go back to earlier days at the Kentucky farm. One summer day the family packed into the car with a picnic lunch and drove across a huge steel truss bridge over the Mississippi River into Missouri, headed for a large park. We went on a tour with a park ranger who explained how this was an important area during the Civil War. The North had pulled a large chain across the Mississippi River here, to prevent Confederate war ships from moving up the river. Later we came across large groups of young men in their late teens or early twenties dressed in simple khaki uniforms. They looked like they might be soldiers, but they were armed with shovels, not guns. The ranger told us they were members of the CCC, the Civilian Conservation Corp. The Corp was designed to give jobs to men without work. I thought I might like to grow up and be a CCC man. They were planting small trees.

While FDR pushed ahead with several bold programs to reduce poverty, he did little to eliminate racial discrimination. Southern Democrats were a large part of his political base and race relations were left to his wife, Eleanor. The main accomplishment I remember was her role in arranging for Marian Anderson, the black contralto, to perform at the Lincoln Memorial when the Daughters of the American Revolution had denied her the opportunity to sing at Constitution Hall. I remember this as a really big deal at the time.

For the most part, the colored didn't participate in the resurgence from the depression. In many ways their conditions worsened. Whites took over many of the jobs that traditionally had gone to the colored: janitors, bus boys, bell boys, and day laborers.

After graduating from the University of Maryland in 1952, I started working for the Navy as a civil engineer. I worked for the David Taylor Model Basin, one of the largest ship model basins in the world, which is located in Cabin John, Maryland, a suburb of Washington, D.C. All the professional workers were white, however, our unit, the Public Works Department, did hire a black architect around 1953. Later I worked for the U. S. Department of Agriculture (USDA) in D.C. doing agricultural research in a unit with a Southern culture. The branch chief was from Georgia and the section head from Mississippi. Employees were recruited from the University of Georgia, University of Alabama, University of South Carolina, and so forth. Our Section Head made it perfectly clear there would be no Negroes in his unit. He was well versed in the agency's administrative rules and regulations and knew how to circumvent them. When I left USDA around 1964 there were still no blacks in his section. This was the year that the Civil Rights Act was passed.

COMMUNIST ATTEMPTS REFORM

They said he was from a famous New York musical family. He was our neighbor in D.C., a late arrival coming in the early 1940s, but Ed Harris was an economist and not a musician. And although he was a PhD, neighborhood kids didn't have to call him Mr. or Dr. Harris. He was an egalitarian and liked to be called Ed. It was the early 1940s, when Ed, his wife, daughter, and two sons moved into the neighborhood. He came to work at the U.S. Department of Agriculture, even though he wasn't a Scandinavian and didn't have a Midwestern or southern farm background like many other USDA officials I knew. Ed was from New York and Jewish.

Ed and his family weren't like the other Jewish family in the neighborhood, the Rosenblatts. Mr. Rosenblatt was short and balding while Ed was tall and thin and had a full head of hair. Everything about the Rosenblatts said Jewish starting with their name. Sonny, their son, went to Hebrew school and Mr. Rosenblatt usually wore a dark suit and always a hat. He wore thick glasses which I envisioned he had to wear from straining his eyes from hours bent over the Torah, reading it in dim light. The Rosenblatts kept all the holidays and dietary codes and didn't associate much with Gentiles. But the Harris's acted like Gentiles, didn't observe Jewish holidays, didn't wear hats, and probably even ate pork. In fact, people said Ed Harris was an atheist, and worse than that, a leftist atheist. In spite of that, he was generally well liked, outgoing, and neighborly, although he sometimes made insulting remarks to neighbors, even children.

On the positive side, Ed was the lone voice of concern for the people of the ghetto. He demonstrated his concern by inviting colored children to his house to play with his children. I could look in his yard from our backyard and see them. They were laughing, squealing, running, and jumping, a sight I'd never seen before. Some suspected Ed brought the colored children to his house just to irritate his white neighbors. But I don't think it worked. For the most part, the neighbors' thinking went like this, "He's just a leftist atheist government bureaucrat and a little crazy, and if he wants his kids playing with the colored, who cares."

Later, Ed faced a lot of tragedy. During the McCarthy era, the mid 1950s, when the House Un-American Activities Committee was operative, Ed was accused of being a Communist and lost his job. I thought, "How exciting, a real live communist in our neighborhood!" By this time I had attended the University of Maryland and been exposed to some of the leftist professors. In fact, in 1948, when I visited Mexico, some students at the National University of Mexico invited me to attend a big political meeting at their school. It was a communist rally—probably for *la Partida Popular Socialista.* Speakers would shout communist' slogans and the audience of students and a few instructors went wild. *"Viva la Partita Socialista!"* they shouted. I questioned the authenticity of this communist leaning audience because they were mostly rich kids and not exploited workers. I'm glad Senator McCarthy never found out that I went to this rally or I might have lost my government job. If he had, my defense would have been, "Senator, but I never cheered once." After the meeting my friends took me on a tour of the near-by red-light district—sightseeing only.

One of our neighbors, Mr. Peterson, wrote a letter to the Department of Agriculture refuting the charges against Ed Harris, saying what a good guy and how all-American Ed was, and how he often sent his kids to Sunday school. My father said, "Ed Harris never sent his children to Sunday school. Peterson was probably just a communist sympathizer himself." For the times, my father was very tolerant of different races, nationalities, and religions, but he hated communism, although he got along fine with Ed Harris.

> *House Un-American Activities Committee finds hot bed of pinko-commie, subversive Bolsheviks and sympathizers infesting quiet Washington suburban neighborhood which is happily situated among majestic oaks and safely away from the swamps of downtown Washington. Reds plot to upset the racial tranquility by integrating the community.*

After a year of unemployment, Ed was reinstated. They found he had only subscribed to some left wing periodical while a graduate student or something similarly benign. What a disappointment, no communists in our community. Ed later divorced his wife. He built a small house for her next to and on the same lot with his house, where he lived with his new wife. He also had a Russian-speaking maid living in his house. Some whispered, "Maybe these living arrangements represent some kind of commune." His daughter, who had schizophrenia, spent time in St. Elizabeths, the large mental hospital in Washington, and eventually committed suicide by taking an overdose of drugs. Some implied these tragedies were because of his leftist atheist leanings and doing things like letting his children play with the colored. In any event, he was the only voice of concern about the plight of the people of the shanty ghetto. Ed eventually left his government job and took a teaching job at a predominantly black college near Philadelphia. Perhaps he was sincere, after all, in his concerns for the people of the shanty ghetto.

5

RETURNING HOME

To the Old Kentucky Home

In November of 1956 I returned to the Kentucky home to visit my uncle and aunts; Grandmother had died several years earlier. My uncle met us at the Paducah airport and drove us to the farm in his Chevy. I guess he couldn't afford a Chrysler since retiring from farming. I came with a wife, a three-year-old son, and a six-month-old baby boy. It had been maybe four or five years since my last visit. My relatives weren't as spry as before and all the farm animals were gone except the chickens. Aunt Alice still took care of the chickens even though she suffered from Parkinson's and shuffled around the chicken yard in quick short steps. My aunts were crazy about my children. Aunt Mollie would reach out eagerly to hold the baby and Aunt Ethel would say, "I just want to sit here and look at you."

The big change was electricity! With the end of the war, TVA and the local rural electrification cooperative had come through with low cost power to the farm. The family had hot and cold running water, a flush toilet, good lighting, a modern refrigerator, an electric stove, reliable phone service, TV, radio, and electric heat in every room. Maybe it was because they'd had the electricity for some time before my visit, that they didn't display much enthusiasm for it. No one said, "Look, here's our new stove!" or "See these great electric heaters in the bedrooms" Maybe it was just the family's stoical tradition or the old saying that anticipation provides more happiness than the event itself. In any case I was excited for them.

My uncle maintained some of his pre-electricity traditions. Before electricity he would go out on the porch with a basin of cold water and shave. This time, on one of the mornings when the temperature was below freezing, he shaved the same way. Even though there was a good electric heater in the living room, he sometimes kept a fire burning in the fireplace. He would stand with his back toward the warm fire, with his hands behind his back, and chew tobacco. From time to time he'd turn around and spit into the fireplace. Our three-year-old would stand with his back towards the fire and spit into the fireplace every time my uncle did.

I felt there was something lost in the new life with electricity. There was a charm about an open wood burning fire, drinking cool water drawn directly from the well, and the family sitting around in the evening swapping stories by the light of a gently glowing kerosene lamp and not all staring fixed and silent on a TV screen. But then like someone has said, "Nostalgia is the past without the pains."

I'm not prepared to counter arguments that critics of the TVA and REA had of the programs, e.g., central planning and subsidies distort the allocation of capital. I don't know to what extent these agencies reduced poverty in the area. Did the benefits exceed the costs? I am convinced, however, that the electricity TVA and REA helped provide, dramatically improved my relatives' lives. It allowed these elderly fragile people to stay in their home. There was no way these folks in their seventies could continue to draw well water and haul it for baths and laundry or cut, split, and haul wood for the stove and fireplace.

I knew in my heart when I said goodbye that I would never see some of these wonderful relatives again, and it wasn't too many years before my aunt Alice died. In addition to the Parkinson's, she had diverticulum of the throat. I often wonder if it wasn't from years of chewing tobacco and in trying to be so discrete about it, that she was swallowing too much tobacco juice.

In 1978 I returned to Marshall County to attend my Uncle Marvin's funeral. He was the last survivor of the folks there. After the burial at the Brewers Methodist church cemetery we drove to the old homestead. We turned off the highway onto the road that took me "home to the place I belong." It was now paved in a ribbon of uniform boring blacktop. It had lost its charm. The homestead had been sold to others and had burned down. Only a barn and corn crib remained. My aunts and uncle were gone, the house was gone, and all the farm animals gone. I thought this would be the end of my visits to the place of sweet comfort, but my wife and I returned again in May, 2013. We came to hear the Big Singing in Benton which I had heard so much about in my early visits to Kentucky. This was the annual community singing of southern harmony that thousands of people attended in earlier years. When I checked in at the motel, there was a problem in getting the room we wanted. I said to the desk clerk, "You must be really busy because of the Big Singing." "What's that?" she said. I thought, "She must be new in the area and just not up on what's going on." The next day, Sunday, I told my wife, "We better leave early so we can get a parking space. We drove to the Benton courthouse; the square was almost empty of people or cars. When we entered the courthouse I was struck by how much better groomed it was than in the 1930s. It was tidy and freshly painted and there were no filthy spittoons in the hallways. The Big Singing took place in a large courtroom that held about one hundred and fifty people, but the room was only half full, and most in attendance were members of the Society for the Preservation of Southern Harmony Singing. We were one of a handful of visitors. What had happened to the special trains and thousands of visitors? We purchased a Southern Harmony song book for $35 so we could sing along following the shape notes. Sheriff Byars stood up and gave a short welcome and then the Society president, Gene Gilliland led out in the first song, *Holy Manna.* Dolores had some success in reading the notes, but I was at a complete loss. While one or two of the hymns were quite moving, the singing was *a capalla* and soon all the songs sounded alike, but the Society members loved it and took turns directing the music.

It was striking that the courthouse squares in Benton, Murray and Mayfield were no longer bustling centers of activities. There were no grocery, hardware, or drugstores, but instead florist shops, real estate offices, and small bookstores. Only a few cars parked on the squares and only a few pedestrians walked the sidewalks. Big-box stores and suburban malls have replaced courthouse square shopping.

WHERE DID THE SHANTY GHETTO CHILDREN GO?

It was on April 12, 1945, that we heard that President Roosevelt had died. It had been just over twelve years since the old fashioned open cockpit bi-planes had flown over our house at his inauguration. My family neither supported nor opposed FDR. We were apolitical. We lived in Washington, D.C., where residents couldn't vote. My father had a Civil Service job and took very seriously the Hatch Act that prevented government employees from engaging in politics. We never had heated discussions around the dinner table about the pros or cons of the president or his politics. After my father retired he did make a few unfavorable remarks about Roosevelt. However, my uncle, in rural Kentucky, was a strong Roosevelt supporter and praised his TVA and REA programs that brought electricity to the farm, and he liked the checks he got in the mail for participating in USDA's agricultural price support program. "People say these are socialistic programs. If they are, then I'm a socialist," he said.

The people of the shanty ghetto still didn't have electricity. They didn't get any USDA or other checks in the mail. Their lot had really not improved much in the twelve years. I guess President Roosevelt didn't want to jeopardize his support from southern Democrats by helping the colored. He left it to Eleanor to champion civil rights.

Soon after the death of the President, WWII ended, and sometime after this, maybe about 1950, the ghetto disappeared. I don't know when it actually happened. It just seemed as though one day the shanties, the woods, and the clay fields were gone and brick duplex homes were standing in their place, occupied by white folks.

In October 1997 when I went back to visit the old neighborhood, I met a man named George coming out of his house. He was living on the next street over from where I used to live. He was wearing shorts, a tee shirt, and no shoes even though it was a cool autumn day. About sixty years old, with a white beard and a pleasant smile and voice, he was one of the few white people on the street. I introduced myself and told him I used to live in the area and wanted to find out more about what had happened to the place since I left it in 1952 when I married Dolores. He told me that he had moved to the neighborhood in 1963, when he was transferred from Detroit to Washington while working for the Food and Drug Administration. We talked a while and he suggested we take a walk around the neighborhood.

As we walked, talking about who had lived where and what had happened to them, George would frequently stop, bend down, and pick up empty aluminum soda cans. He was like many of the new Takoma Park breed, interested in recycling, saving the environment, and banning the bomb. Bumper stickers in the area read, "Save the Whales," or "Save the Wilderness," or "Animals are not ours to eat, wear, or experiment with."

Most of the people I had known had already left or died by the time George had moved in, but he had known Ed Harris. "Everyone knew Ed Harris," he said with a smile. George had also known both of Ed's wives. Ed had continued to live in the neighborhood while teaching at the black college in Pennsylvania. After Ed's death in 1970, his first wife went to New York to be near her sons; his second wife continued living in the old house, but recently had gone to a nursing home.

Most of the old homes were still intact and in good shape. There had been a period in the late 1960s and 1970s when housing seemed to deteriorate in Takoma Park. On this sunny day in October with bright colorful foliage, things looked good. However, the houses, the trees, the yards, the walls didn't look as big as they did when I was a kid. And in fact, some of the large lots that held fine large homes had been subdivided and another smaller house built on the new lot. Many of the majestic oaks had been cut down to accommodate the new house. A few of the lawns and gardens weren't as neat as the old days. For example, some were like George's place. George was into the natural look; he had no lawn, just a yard overgrown with trees, bushes, flowers, and weeds.

I told George that in about 1955, the neighborhood was still all white when my parents moved to Florida. This was a time when blacks were starting to move into white neighborhoods. Stories were rampant about how real estate values would plummet if the street went black. First, one black family would move on a street, something called "block busting." A precedent was set. The old covenants that prevented selling to blacks were being challenged. Whites often panicked and sold out and soon the entire block would turn black. By panicking, the whites helped to make the prophecy of declining home prices come true. At one time there was a coalition of blacks and whites in Washington that tried to discourage neighborhoods from going all black, to keep housing prices up and stop the creation of new ghettos.

My parents agonized about whether they should sell to blacks. They didn't want to be the first. Like many other whites in this situation, they solved the problem by selling to a white real estate broker who in turn sold to blacks. It cost them several thousand dollars to do it this way, but they felt they hadn't betrayed their neighbors. A few white families like the Harris's, however, stuck it out and stayed on living there with the black "invasion."

When George moved into the neighborhood in 1963, the streets with older homes were mostly inhabited by white, but the newer, smaller brick duplex homes built after World War II were now all occupied by blacks. Over time more and more blacks moved into the older homes. In 1997 the neighborhood was about 75 percent black. The Adventist church had moved their headquarters and publishing house out of Takoma Park. USDA was downsizing and decentralizing by moving to regional offices. Employees of these institutions no longer dominated the neighborhood. A new breed of government worker was moving in after 1963, working for new agencies such as the Environmental Protection Agency or the National Oceanic and Atmospheric Administration.

George told me, when he first moved to Takoma Park, there were few social relations between the races, but over time some strong friendships had developed. However, the brick duplex houses were all occupied by blacks, and there was little contact between either whites or blacks of the older neighborhood and the people of the new duplex homes. So, in a sense, the old shanty ghetto had been replaced by a new brick duplex ghetto.

As we walked the streets and talked, I could see how my old neighborhood had changed. The old neighborhood, segregated, austere, proper, and blind to the squalor and injustice, had been replaced by an integrated one, more tolerant, more progressive, with an unconventional or hippie-like lifestyle. The houses which were large for their time now seemed smaller and had lost some of their past glory. The area which was crime free and safe when I had lived there, was now suffering from petty crimes such as car thefts, break-ins, and old cars left abandoned on the streets. But my tour with George was more than sixteen years ago and today crime seems to have decreased and much of the hippie lifestyle is gone.

George and I walked up to the edge of a large bank where the clay fields used to be and now there were industrial buildings. The fine old three-story Victorian Lamond home which stood at the top of the clay banks was gone. George told me it had gone through a period of severe decay and finally was torn down. I pointed down the street with the brick duplex homes and told him that's where the colored shanties used to be. He didn't know about them. I showed him where the water hydrant used to be where the colored got all their water.

As I stood there I wondered what had happened to the people of the shanty ghetto. I remember when the colored children limped along my old street, when the domestics served in our homes, and the old colored men stood around watching the women boil clothes in black cast iron kettles over wood fires. Who knows what has happened to them? They may have gotten many civil rights in the 1960s, but their bodies and minds had probably already been damaged by inadequate diets. Their schooling had stopped at the fourth grade; college scholarships for minorities wouldn't have helped. These things had all come too late for them.

One thing I really regret is that with a few exceptions I did not speak to or even recognize the children of the ghetto. I greeted neighborhood dogs with "nice doggie" or cats with "here kitty, kitty." The ghetto children I mostly ignored. And like the other children as well as the adults in our neighborhood, I treated the colored ghetto children not just as subhuman beings but as inanimate objects.

Today Takoma Park promotes itself as a suburban community with "newcomers of all races and nationalities living side by side." There are interracial couples in the town and even a few same gender couples. The churches and most community groups are integrated. On the Maryland side most schools are largely integrated, but the schools on the District side of Takoma Park are mostly black. People are concerned about the poor performance of District schools. Few young couples with children, either white or black, want to move to the District side. Some that did are experimenting with home schooling

In the 1930s, about twenty five percent of D.C. residents were black. It was a southern segregated city and the blacks knew "their place." There was little talk of civil rights or reform, and whites didn't feel threatened by them. I heard few derogatory remarks about blacks; they were mostly ignored. While I mentioned the "No Jews or Italians" sign, I actually heard very few disparaging remarks about them either, although our Presbyterian next door neighbor apologized to my mother for selling their house to Catholics. The Catholic family, which had four fine sons, turned out to be a great neighbor.

In rural western Kentucky in the 1930s most everyone was white Anglo Saxon and Protestant (WASPs). Blacks, Catholics, Jews, and southern Europeans were so few, the WASPs ignored them. I never heard ethnic slurs about them, but we have seen how a Confederate shadow loomed over the land. Even today it's largely a WASP area and we can only speculate the extent blacks and other minorities would suffer discrimination if there were a significant number. However, the severe rural poverty is gone and there is electricity. Instead of small tobacco farms, you see large prosperous farms growing corn, soybeans, and wheat. No mule teams cultivate the fields. You see huge green high tech farm machines trimmed in yellow and with a yellow deer emblem—tractors, combines, and chemical applicators that cost several hundred thousand dollars each.

I don't believe minorities or the rural poor in Kentucky, or even most blacks in D.C., suffered like the people of the black shanty ghetto near our house. Over my lifetime the worst bigotry and poverty I ever witnessed was in this shanty ghetto. Families were living in one-room poorly heated shacks, with inadequate diets that led to rickets, no medical care, few educational opportunities, and no warm winter clothes. I was just a kid then, didn't understand, and didn't care. This was just the way things were. As time went on I saw more racial bigotry and discrimination. As a sixteen year old I witnessed how the Reconstruction Finance Corporation where I worked manipulated job titles to keep blacks out of the better paying positions, and still I didn't really see the injustice. Grownups were running things and they must have known what was best. As a twenty year old I saw the separate but unequal bus stations in Mississippi, Tennessee, and Louisiana and I saw the black lady shoved to the back of the bus to sit on an overcrowded bench seat. This injustice did register with me. When I was in my early thirties, I witnessed USDA officials cleverly avoiding equal rights regulations to keep blacks out of the workplace. But I didn't do anything about these problems. I'm not a real proactive reformer and wouldn't feel comfortable participating in civil rights marches. I've volunteered as a mentor for disadvantaged black children through a black church and the D.C. court system, and I've worked on housing and community development programs for minorities and the poor for the state of Connecticut, where I was Chief of Research and Program Evaluation for the Department of Community Affairs. But I don't claim to have done much in my life for the cause of justice for all races. I try to treat people of all ethnicities with respect. I have two great-grandchildren and both are of mixed race—one Asian-American and one Mexican-American and I couldn't be more proud of them. Believe me, having descendants of a different race will soften your heart towards other races. I feel minorities should also be tolerant of majorities and not look for the worst in them. My friend Arthur, who is black, told this story: "I was sitting in church near a white man. It was near the beginning of the service and the minister asked us to greet those near us. You know, say something like, 'peace be with you.' I turned towards the white man extending my hand but he ignored me. I thought he's just a bigot and won't greet me because I'm black. Then I noticed a red and white cane next to him. He was blind."

My story started about a sign prohibiting Jews and Italians at a Chesapeake Bay beach, and then I wrote mostly about bigotry against blacks in my Washington, D.C. neighborhood and rural life and poverty in western Kentucky. Now I end with an American Indian prayer. Maybe the narrative is rambling and inconsistent, but it's the story I wanted to tell and I close with a final news bulletin:

> *Little white trash, spoiled, racially insensitive kid with thick glasses
> and sissy pants grows up to cite prayer of North American
> Sioux calling for racial harmony and understanding.*

Grandfather Great Spirit

All over the world the faces of living ones are alike.

With tenderness they have come up out of the ground.

Give us the strength to understand, and the eyes to see.

Teach us to walk the soft Earth as relatives to all that live.[2]

---

[2] There are several versions of this prayer in both printed form (Elizabeth Roberts and Elias Amidon, Eds., Earth Prayers, 1991) and on native American and other web sites (search for Sioux prayers, With tenderness they have come up, or As relatives to all that live).

ACKNOWLEDGEMENTS

While this book is based largely on my experiences and observations, it would not have been possible without the help of many people.

First, I want to thank Dolores, my wife of 62 years, for reading and commenting on the many drafts of the book, helping find photographs, and verifying facts and figures. I imposed on neighbors, friends, and relatives to review my manuscript, and they generously obliged giving me valuable and insightful comments. They include: Robert & Ellen Nixon, Louise Bindseil, Barry Casey, Janet Davis, Lucy Walker, and Carolyn Joanne McFarland. Laura Oliver, a prize winning author and creative writing teacher, provided great advice and comments.

I want to give special recognition to Mr. Clair Garman, who produced the maps. Robert Bouland, my youngest son, provided tech support. Others who helped include: Diana Kohn, Historic Takoma Inc.; Ken Rucker, National Trolley Museum; Laura Barry, Historical Society of Washington, D.C. Library; Derek Gray, Martin Luther King Library; Deana Wright, Murray Main Street; and Dorothy Barnes, long time citizen of Takoma Park.

ABOUT THE AUTHOR

Heber Bouland was born in Washington, D.C. in 1928 and resided there for twenty four years. Most of his adult life he has lived in the Maryland suburbs of D.C. Much of his career has been in analyzing community, housing, and economic development programs for the U.S. General Accounting Office and the Connecticut Department of Community Affairs. He also directed relief and development projects in Africa, Central America, and the Philippines. After his retirement he wrote a coffee-table book, *Barns across America.* He resides in Columbia, Maryland with his wife, Dolores.

CPSIA information can be obtained
at www.ICGtesting.com
Printed in the USA
LVOW04s0056170817

545328LV00007B/35/P